TOWARDS THE HARMONIZATION OF IMMIGRATION AND REFUGEE LAW IN SADC

**Jonathan Klaaren and
Bonaventure Rutinwa**

MIDSA Report No 1

Editor: Prof. Jonathan Crush

Published by Idasa, 6 Spin Street, Church Square, Cape Town, 8001, and Queen's University, Canada.

Copyright Southern African Migration Project (SAMP) 2004
ISBN 1-919798-72-2
ISBN-13: 978 1 919798 72 1
First published 2004
Design by Unwembi Communications
Typeset in RotisSemiSerif 10pt

Printed by Lighning Source

TABLE OF CONTENTS

Chapter Four: Immigration Law and Policy 52

Chapter Five: Refugees and Immigration Controls 78

LIST OF TABLES

EDITORIAL NOTE

In August 2001, at the First Forum of the Migration Dialogue for Southern Africa (MIDSA) in Ezulwini, Swaziland, the member states resolved that MIDSA should undertake a regional, SADC-wide scope of citizenship, migration, immigration and refugee legislation. As the primary research and policy agency within MIDSA, the Southern African Migration Project (SAMP) undertook this task. A research proposal was tabled and approved by the delegates at the 2nd MIDSA Forum in Gaberone, Botswana, in February 2002. The information-gathering component of the study involved two phases: (a) collection of legislation, regulations and other relevant documentation for all SADC states. Copies of this information are available for consultation at the University of the Witwatersrand and the Southern African Research Centre at Queen's University; and (b) interviews with key informants in relevant government departments in 12 SADC states (Appendix A). Following their research, the texts and interviews were subject to a close legal reading and analysis by the two legal consultants responsible for this report, Professor Bonaventure Rutinwa of the University of Dar-es-Salaam and Professor Jonathan Klaaren of the University of the Witwatersrand. The researchers conducted research in all but one SADC state. The researchers, SAMP and the MIDSA partners would like to express their sincere thanks to all of the officials who facilitated country-visits by the researchers, provided them with documentation, and generously gave of their time to discuss the issues covered in this report. SAMP would also like to express its gratitude to the International Organisation for Migration (IOM), the Canadian International Development Agency (CIDA) and the Bureau for Population, Refugees and Migration (PRM) for their support of this project.

Authors

Jonathan Klaaren is an asssociate professor of Law at the University of Witwatersrand. Bonaventure Rutinwa is senior lecturer in Law at the University of Dar-es-Salaam.

EXECUTIVE SUMMARY

The MIDSA project on legal harmonization of immigration and refugee law in the Southern African Development Community had four main objectives: (a) to collect and collate information on national legislation in a single publication as a resource for policy-makers; (b) to identify points of similarity and difference in national immigration law between SADC-member states; (c) to investigate the possibilities for harmonization of national immigration policy and law; and (d) in the interests of good governance and regional cooperation and integration to make specific recommendations for harmonization. A second, parallel, SAMP study is investigating the issue of harmonization of migration data collection systems within SADC.

For ease of inter-country comparison, the report contains a series of comparative tables covering all facets of the immigration regime of the SADC states. The tables can be used as a resource in themselves but are also used to supplement the analysis in the text proper. This executive summary focuses on the main findings and recommendations of the narrative report.

The states of the SADC have committed themselves to increased regional cooperation and integration. This commitment is reflected in a series of Protocols to which the various states are signatory. The Protocol dealing with the cross-border migration of people within SADC (the so-called "Draft Free Movement Protocol") owed too much to European (Schengen) precedent and too little to the political and economic realities of the region. As a result, the Protocol (and a modified version called the "Facilitation of Movement Protocol") was rejected by certain states in the region (primarily the migrant-receiving states). The level of opposition was such that the Protocol was shelved by SADC in 2000.

While this publication is not designed to promote or contest the idea of free movement, it is the belief of the MIDSA partners that good migration governance is a general aim to which all can subscribe. To that end it makes perfect sense for the individual states of SADC to re-examine their current legislation. Migration has changed dramatically in the last decade and a review of the adequacy of existing legal and policy instruments would be a positive development for all states. Beyond the issue of updating legislation and making it more relevant to current management challenges, it is clear that regional cooperation in migration management would be facilitated by a set of basic principles and laws that applied more-or-less across the region. Obviously each country has certain unique features and each state reserves the right to pursue its own immigration policy. However, there are many features of migration governance that are common to all and there is nothing to be lost, and a great deal to be gained, by simplification and standardization.

A regional review of this nature also allows for an analysis of the degree to which individual states have been influenced by or subscribe to international conventions and norms in the migration and refugee protection areas. A secondary purpose of this publication is therefore to stimulate a regional debate on the extent to which individual SADC states do or should adhere to the principles of international conventions and guidelines on the movement of peoples and the protection of the persecuted.

The report itself is divided into five separate thematic chapters. The first three chapters consider issues that are foundational to the efficient working of any immigration regime: citizenship and registration law. The final two chapters focus more centrally on immigration and refugee law. These are the meat of the report. However, it is argued that harmonization of practices and standards in the first two areas would not only improve and simplify management but would also facilitate the process of harmonizing immigration, migration and refugee law. This summary therefore follows the structure of the report as a whole by presenting the major findings and recommendations under each heading.

Citizenship

- The citizenship laws of the countries of the SADC region can be considered as part of the migration regulation regimes of those countries. As part of the migration regime of a country, laws of citizenship provide for a form of membership. The legal status of "citizen" is higher than the status of a permanent resident (where that category exists), temporary resident, refugee or unauthorized migrant.

- Domestic laws of citizenship are subject to few international standards. There are some modest protections, mostly extending to married women and to children. Domestic laws of citizenship are, however, subject to constitutional standards. Mauritius, Namibia, Zambia, and Zimbabwe have constitutions that contain detailed rules regarding citizenship. Other countries in SADC have legislation providing detailed rules regarding citizenship.

- The laws of citizenship in the SADC countries are relatively stable. Other than Mauritius, South Africa, Tanzania, and Zimbabwe, all citizenship legislation is at least ten years old. Lesotho and Zimbabwe are the only countries demonstrating current legislative change in their citizenship policies.

- There are five significant routes to acquiring citizenship in the countries of SADC: birth, descent, and naturalization as well as marriage and registration. The right to citizenship based upon birth in the territory is relatively limited in SADC, despite the legal tradition of many of these countries from the British Commonwealth where the right of *jus soli* existed (right to citizenship based on birth).

- In contrast, the right to citizenship of children of citizens is generally accepted throughout SADC. Every country in SADC provides some form of the right to citizenship based on descent, *jus sanguinis*. Nonetheless, six countries limit this right with respect to territory of birth, some further limit the right by means of registration or choice of nationality requirements, and four countries impose limitations on citizen parents' ability to pass on citizenship to their children.

- For the second generation of children born abroad, the situations of Malawi and Mauritius are substantially different from the rest of the SADC region. Neither Malawi nor Mauritius allows for children born abroad of a parent who is a citizen by descent to receive citizenship.

- There are important differences in respect of residence requirements and knowledge of national language, as well as other features. Most countries of the SADC region require applicants for naturalization to renounce any prior citizenship in order to be eligible for a new citizenship. There are two clear exceptions to the requirement of renunciation at naturalization: Botswana and South Africa. Residence requirements range between five and ten years. Knowledge of the languages or culture of the naturalizing country is a common but not universal requirement in SADC.

- Almost all the SADC countries have separate provisions relating to the acquisition of citizenship by a spouse married to a national. These separate provisions for foreign spouses are uniformly less onerous than the provisions for naturalization. Zambia is the sole exception, using its system of citizenship by registration to regulate the acquisition of citizenship by "alien" spouses. Some countries demonstrate a concern with the length of the marriage, using this requirement to distinguish between genuine marriages and marriages of convenience.

- The acquisition of citizenship by registration is a residual or catch-all category that essentially differs country by country. Citizenship by registration is a mode of acquisition often with respect to adoptions and minor children.

- The issue of dual citizenship is explicitly treated in the citizenship laws of most of the SADC countries. Using a specific test of "relative tolerance," it emerges that the countries of the SADC region are almost evenly divided on the relative tolerance of dual citizenship. Five countries either explicitly prohibit dual citizenship or have a rule that mandates loss of citizenship upon even involuntary or marriage-based acquisition of a foreign citizenship. Seven countries have policies that are relatively tolerant.

- There is a remarkable uniformity in the policies of SADC countries with respect to loss/deprivation of citizenship. In almost all instances, provisions with respect to loss of citizenship apply only to citizens by registration or naturalization. The rule is that extended absence in a foreign country without notification can result in loss of citizenship. There is perhaps most variation around the loss of citizenship on account of a criminal conviction.

- The policy on reacquisition of citizenship in SADC is flexible and facilitative. There are nearly no limits on what classes of citizens may apply for reacquisition.

- In most of the SADC laws of citizenship (but not all), formal documentary proof of citizenship is identified. In almost all the countries of SADC, the implementing institution for immigration law is the same as that for citizenship law.

Population Registration and Identification

- By facilitating the identification of persons, registration and identification of persons a country is better equipped to secure its borders and protect exclusive rights of citizens without prejudicing non-citizens working, visiting, trading or receiving asylum in the country. Some laws in SADC deal with registration and identification separately while others cover the two under one statute.

- The majority of countries make the registration of persons mandatory and impose the obligation on either the individuals to register themselves or specified officers to maintain population registers.

- There are two main procedures for registration. The first is by way of application by the persons to whom the registration provisions apply. The second main procedure is by way of information for the population register being compiled by a specified public official from any appropriate source.

- The particulars to be included in the register which are common in most laws are: national identity number where applicable, the full name, residential address, sex, date of birth, place of birth, occupation, postal address, marital status and full/maiden name of spouse and other particulars relating to marital status.

- Some laws empower the registration authorities to request any person to furnish proof of the correctness of any particulars which have been furnished in respect of such person in any documents for the purposes of registration. Generally, the laws do not allude to the evidential value of the contents of registers except in relation to the probative value of certificates produced and issued on the basis of the contents of registers

- The principal way by which the identity of persons is ascertained is by production of identification documents specifically designed for that purpose or any other secondary documents acceptable to serve for that purpose. In SADC, the primary means of identification is an "Identity Document" or "Identity Card" issued after prescribed procedures have been exhausted. In some countries, the other documents that are acceptable as secondary forms include passports and drivers licences.

- Even where it is not compulsory to possess an identity document, persons may be compelled to apply for the same depending on the uses for which the identity documents may be required. The first and foremost requirement for obtaining identity documents is that a person must be eligible to register under the relevant law and must have so registered. The statutory procedures for issuance of identity documents differ slightly from country to country.

- Some statutes expressly specify the particulars that must be contained in the identity documents while others simply confer upon the relevant Minister the obligation to determine what the content of identity documents should be. The common contents of identity documents are: identity number, full name, date and place of birth, citizenship status, photograph of the person concerned and fingerprints. Others are colour of eyes, height of the person concern, the region of origin and place of application for registration.

- While nationality is often included, this does not mean that identity documents are necessarily a conclusive proof of migration status, or indeed, of any other of their contents. The probative value given to identity cards differs from one country to another. Because they are obtained after producing identity documents, travel documents (such as passports) are acceptable in many countries as alternative or secondary means of identification.

- A number of laws make provisions requiring the production of identity documents when so required by competent officers. Identity documents are required not only for identification purposes, but also as a precondition for receiving certain services provided by the state.

Registration of Births and Deaths

- The registration of births and deaths plays an important role in immigration regimes. Most of the details which are recorded at birth such as date, place of birth and parentage are very crucial to issues of citizenship and identification which in turn are critical to movement-related rights, namely the right to enter, remain and leave a country. The registration of deaths facilitates the enforcement of the provisions of registration and identification laws which require identity documents of deceased persons to be surrendered, preventing their misuse.

- In some countries, registration of births is compulsory for everyone. In others, registration of births is not compulsory except for prescribed persons or in described geographical areas. The limitation of compulsory registration requirements to persons of certain races only is found in a couple of laws that are fairly old, applying the duty to persons who are not indigenous.

- The laws require separate registers of births to be maintained in which prescribed details are recorded. These details as well as the form in which they are to be presented are normally provided for in regulations or rules made under the principal legislation.

- The right, or the duty (where registration is compulsory), to register a birth of a child born alive is primarily imposed on its father or mother. In the absence or inability of the father or mother, any person present at the birth including medical personnel, an occupier of dwellings where a child was born or any person having charge of the child, must give notice. If a birth has not been registered within twelve months, it can only be registered with the permission of the prescribed officer, usually the highest registration authority.

- All legislation makes provisions for children born out of wedlock, who under some legislation are referred to as "illegitimate children." The requirement for a separate procedure for registration of children born of unmarried couples is intended to avoid creating paternity disputes, which in some jurisdictions have occurred.

- The laws allow the registered names to be changed in specified circumstances and upon application by specified persons.

- Death registers are usually maintained at two main levels: the national level and the district level, where a death register is maintained by a district registrar, who is required to enter therein every death occurring within the district whereof particulars have been reported to him or her.

- Some countries have a compulsory registration of deaths; others limit this duty geographically or by population (as with births). The laws set time periods after which registration of a death must follow a different procedure for "late registration."

- The common information which is required to be supplied for the purposes of registering a death include: serial/entry number; name and surname of the deceased; age; sex; full address/residence; nationality; profession or occupation of the deceased; date, place and cause of death; and the signature, full name, address and profession or occupation of the informant and the signature of the registering officer. Different laws assign different evidential value to death certificates.

Immigration and Migration

- There has been relatively recent change in SADC migration laws. At least five countries have significantly changed their migration laws within the past ten years: Mozambique, Namibia, South Africa, Tanzania, and Zimbabwe. Presently, the South African situation is in transition and Lesotho is in the midst of a fundamental revision of its statute.

- There are few multilateral international instruments that appear to be incorporated or used to any great extent in the migration regimes of the countries of SADC. Relevant international instruments that regulate the treatment of migrant workers and their families and international instruments that regulate international trade and services have not been adopted. Instead, a number of bilateral international agreements appear to play an important role in the functioning of migration regimes in the SADC region. Operational agreements may also exist at the bilateral level. Further, there are regular bilateral committee meetings at the operational level.

- At the present time, there appears to be little or no prospect of revival of the 1995 SADC Draft Protocol on Free Movement. However, a number of SADC Protocols contain provisions that are relevant to migration within the region such as that on Education and Training and the one on Immunities and Privileges. There is also some reference to the special position of the Southern African Development Community in national migration regimes.

- In general, SADC countries do not differ significantly in the grounds of exclusion that they adopt, at least within countries that come within the British legal tradition. The categories of exclusion include economic grounds, disease, a past criminal conviction, national security, and prior violation of a migration law. Four countries had no explicit ground for exclusion based on prostitution or living on the proceeds of prostitution, but six others do. Malawi and Zimbabwe specify status as a homosexual as a grounds for exclusion. With respect to the effect of these grounds of exclusion, South Africa distinguishes between their automatic and discretionary impact and their impact on temporary and permanent residence.

- The temporary residence permit systems of the SADC countries differ in regards to their specificity. The South African system is the most specific with fifteen different categories. A general permit can substitute for specific permits, although it does not serve to communicate the policy aims of the more specific categories. All countries have some type of visitor's or general-purpose permit, with limits ranging from 90 days to 12 months.

- Many of the SADC countries have specific temporary residence permits for study or educational purposes; few have permits implementing international agreements or for specific health purposes. Many of the SADC countries have specific permits for the entrance of relatives. Only South Africa provides specific statutory authority for retired persons' permits, international exchange permits, and cross-border passes. Some SADC countries still issue the temporary permit to a prohibited person.

- Five SADC countries have legislation granting employment permits separate from their migration legislation. Even where there is no separate legislation, there may be involvement by a separate institution in decisions regarding employment permits.

- In most SADC countries, visas are a necessary but not a sufficient condition to enter. In some countries, visas function as temporary permits for either all or some categories of temporary residence.

- In deciding on temporary employment permits, SADC countries consider the effect on domestic employment, the condition of pre-entry engagement for employment, the limitation of a permit to a specific employer, the condition that the worker be paid a prevailing wage, and the condition that the employer undertake specific training arrangements. Some countries may limit the geographic area of the employment permit.

- At least eight SADC countries have specific policies designed to attract investors or those persons with significant financial resources.

- Currently operative bilateral labour agreements govern labour migration between South Africa on the one side and Mozambique, Botswana, Lesotho, and Swaziland on the other. These agreements also provide for repatriation and readmission of unauthorized entrants. These agreements will need to be renegotiated in light of South Africa's Immigration Act.

- There is a fair amount of variation in the permanent residence policies of the SADC region; Swaziland does not have this category at all. One model treats permanent residence as an extension of temporary status; the other distinguishes sharply between temporary and permanent residents. In both models, permanent residence status can either be an automatic or a discretionary decision. If it is automatic, permanent residence is usually dependent either on years of lawful status (ranging from five to ten years) or on family status.

- There is significant variety within the SADC countries regarding the procedures provided for exclusion (refusal to grant admission). Nonetheless, for almost all the countries, there is a basic minimum requirement of written notification of the action of exclusion to the person who is excluded. A common but not universal second element of the usual exclusion procedures in the SADC countries is the opportunity to receive a provisional permit. A third element of the national exclusion procedures commonly used is the opportunity for representations to the Minister, generally within three days. A fourth element of exclusion procedures is the possibility of an appearance in or an appeal to the court structures. However, the immigration laws of some countries explicitly preclude or substantially limit appeal to a court.

- The international requirement of a procedure established by law for expulsion or deportation is probably met by all the SADC countries, though shortfalls exist in many countries with respect to the public availability of laws, regulations, and procedures. Tanzania, Swaziland, and Zambia come closest to the international minimum standards, apparently requiring only notification or warrants for some of those persons subject to expulsion. Other countries specify either additional internal administrative or additional external judicial procedures or both.

- The relationship between exclusion grounds and procedures and the grounds and procedures for expulsion are close in a number of SADC countries. This linkage is often due to the category of status as a prohibited immigrant.

- Only two SADC countries have the same statutory rules to govern detention at the border and detention pending expulsion: Lesotho and South Africa. Most of the MIDSA countries specify a relatively short period of time for detention of persons at the border (around 14 days). The location of detention may vary. In many SADC migration statutes, a bond may be paid in place of detention for persons who are arrested at the border. Often, the period of time allowed for detention pending expulsion is not specified.

- Generally there is relatively light regulation—essentially monitoring—of departures from SADC countries of both citizens and non-citizens, the potential exception being Malawi.

- There is not a great variety in the offences identified and punished in the migration laws of SADC. The distinction between administrative offences and criminal offences is made explicitly only in Mozambique (via the Code) and in South Africa.

- There is no specific criminalization of trafficking in the national legislation of the SADC region. However, criminal offences are provided for that come close to elements of the crime of trafficking. The closest typical offence is that of aiding and abetting the unlawful entry of persons. Trafficking is an area of law and policy where the twin vulnerabilities of gender and migration are most apparent.

- Xenophobia is becoming a significant social problem, though it is typically perceived to be present nearly exclusively in South Africa. In fact, levels of intolerance and acceptance vary from country to country and between different socio-economic groups within countries. Antagonism is growing in Botswana and Namibia.

- Considering gender issues, most officials emphasized simply that there was no formal discrimination: "just the same, no special treatment." However, the dual vulnerabilities of gender and migration mean that gender neutral policies may often impact negatively more on women than on men. Most of the countries under study felt that changes in the law were necessary to deal with marriages of convenience, although there was no consensus on the direction that should be taken.

- The police, and to a lesser extent, the defence force and prisons services are used in implementing the immigration laws. Labour agencies are often involved either formally or informally in employment permits. Angola and Mozambique differ significantly from other SADC countries in having a substantial government body that is competent to deal with the affairs of their citizens abroad. South Africa has the legal authority to privatize some of its migration implementation.

- Most countries of the SADC were legally empowered to recover costs of repatriation from carriers, but only South Africa was authorized to levy a financial sanction on the carrier or had more extensive cost recovery provisions.

Migration Control and Refugee Protection

- For a number of reasons, the quality of refugee legislation has an impact on the efficiency of immigration regimes. The overwhelming majority of SADC countries have ratified the key international instruments relating to refugees and have enacted legislation to deal with the phenomenon.

- The international instruments of refugees, as complemented by human rights treaties, enshrine the principles of asylum and *non-refoulement*, principles that have implications for migration controls. Additionally, the principle of protection guarantees to refugees minimum standards of treatment with respect to freedom of movement, gainful employment, and equality of treatment. States also have a duty to find durable solutions to the plight of refugees by way of either repatriation, resettlement or local integration. Finally, the principle of international co-operation enjoins states to co-operate in addressing refugee problems.

- There are two main ways by which refugees are defined under various SADC legislation. The first approach, found in more modern legislation, is to provide a specific definition of a refugee, usually, the definition under the 1951 UN Convention on refugees and the 1969 OAU Convention on refugees in Africa. The second approach, found mainly in legislation enacted in the 1970s (Swaziland and Zambia), is to simply vest the powers to determine who is a refugee in the Minister responsible for refugee affairs.

- Some SADC legislation extends the list of persons excludable from refugee status beyond the usual list of the definition. Some countries exclude persons from safe third countries.

- The immigration legislation of all SADC countries requires non-citizens to obtain permission to enter the territories of countries of which they are not nationals. While refugee laws do not remove this requirement as such, they exempt refugees from the consequences of not complying with it. Much SADC refugee legislation expressly protects asylum seekers from being penalised for illegal entry or presence.

- A prima facie declaration is conclusive as to the status of all members of the class of persons so declared. The countries whose laws have such a provision are Lesotho, South Africa, Swaziland, Tanzania, Zambia and Zimbabwe.

- Individualised procedures for status determination are found under the laws of Angola, Botswana, Namibia, Lesotho, Malawi, Mozambique, South Africa, Tanzania and Zimbabwe, as well as (administratively) in Zambia.

- In virtually all countries, a person who wishes to be recognised as a refugee must present himself or herself to specified government authorities in the area of entry and indicate his or her desire to apply for asylum.

- The body charged to hear applications for asylum is an inter-ministerial Committee typically drawing membership from the Departments of Refugees, Immigration, Police, Security, Ministry of Foreign Affairs and the Officer of the President. In a few countries, the Ministries of Education, Labour and Social Affairs are also represented. UNHCR is also represented in an observer capacity.

- With regard to appeals and reviews, the procedures to be followed depend on the level at which the first decision is made and whether or not the procedure followed is administrative or quasi-judicial.

- There is considerable difference in the laws and practices of various countries with regard to freedom of movement by refugees. About half of the SADC countries require refugees to reside in specified refugee settlements. Refugees are not allowed to leave these settlements without permits unless they have expressly been exempted. The other half either explicitly or in practice allow freedom of movement. A number of laws make provisions for granting refugees identity and travel documents.

- The laws and practices of SADC countries differ on wage-earning employment. A few countries have provisions that make it possible for refugees to be naturalised in those countries. A few exclude this possibility and others are silent on the issue.

1 ☒ CITIZENSHIP LAWS IN SADC

INTRODUCTION

This chapter surveys the citizenship laws of the Southern African Development Community (SADC) countries. In one sense, the laws relating to citizenship should hardly be the topic of a report; citizenship laws arguably themselves constitute the nation.[1] By linking the nation to the individual, citizenship laws are often among the most "political" of laws. For instance, in South Africa, apartheid laws that made black citizens into aliens in the land of their birth were among the most hated and contested.[2] Likewise, in Mozambique, the Nationality Law of June 1975 entered into force at the same precise time as the Constitution.[3] Officially, the Nationality Law is described as "one of the politico-legal instruments which enshrine the total and complete independence of the Mozambican people."[4]

The chapter does not consider the laws of citizenship in this political and national expressive sense. Instead, this chapter considers the laws of citizenship as part of the migration regime of a country. As such, laws of citizenship regulate the closest form of membership in a country. The status of citizen is higher than that of permanent resident (if that category exists), temporary resident or unauthorized migrant.[5]

The laws of citizenship form part of the migration regime in at least two ways. First, the laws of citizenship define who are the nationals of a country. Thus, the laws of citizenship also define who are not nationals of a country. These are persons who are non-citizens; otherwise known as "aliens" or "foreigners." Nationals of a country usually have certain rights, including the right to return to or enter the country. Non-citizens usually do not enjoy the right to enter a country and usually can only enter the country under certain conditions of temporary or permanent residence. Thus, the laws of citizenship are important to show who is subject to the migration regulation.

Second, laws of citizenship give the rules for persons to access the fullest membership of a country. A person is most fully integrated (at least in a legal sense) into the country when he or she is a citizen of that country. Citizenship is thus an important status for integration of immigrants into a country. The laws of citizenship have rules for access to citizenship.

For the most part, domestic laws of citizenship are not subject to international legal norms. This is because part of a state's sovereignty is the right to determine its own laws of citizenship. However, citizenship does have some functions in international law. In terms of international law, a state has a right to protect its nationals in relation to other states. Additionally, a national has a right to be admitted to and to reside in the territory of the state of nationality.

Furthermore, there are some 'modest' limitations to a country's nationality policy in terms of international law.[6] Article 1 of the 1957 Convention on the Nationality of Married Women provides that "neither the celebration nor the dissolution of a marriage between one of its nationals and an alien, nor change of nationality by the husband, shall automatically affect the nationality of the wife." Article 2 provides that "neither the voluntary acquisition of the nationality of another State nor the renunciation of its nationality by one of its nationals shall prevent the retention of its nationality by the wife of such national." Article 1 of the 1961 Convention on the Reduction of Statelessness obligates a contracting state to "grant its nationality to a person born in its territory who would otherwise be stateless." Article 7 provides some protection against loss of citizenship for those citizens seeking nationality elsewhere through naturalization processes. Other international instruments provide for non-discrimination on grounds of race and gender. In particular, there is an independent right to nationality on behalf of children in Article 7(1) of the 1989 Rights of the Child Convention.

The ultimate source for a country's governing law on citizenship will usually rest with its constitution. However, in practice and particularly with respect to migration, the rules relating to citizenship are put into place in legislation. The constitutions of several countries do contain detailed rules regarding citizenship: Mauritius, Mozambique,[7] Namibia, Zambia, and Zimbabwe. Other than with respect to these countries, we did not focus on the rules of citizenship as expressed in constitutions. Instead, we researched the rules of citizenship as expressed in legislation. Table 1 identifies the primary sources of rules for citizenship for each SADC country.

Generally, one can observe that the laws of citizenship in the SADC countries are relatively stable. Other than Mauritius, South Africa, Tanzania,[8] and Zimbabwe, all citizenship legislation is at least ten years old.[9] Furthermore, even though it was a post-apartheid law, the 1995 South African citizenship law made surprisingly few changes to the preceeding legislation.[10] Mauritius amended its citizenship laws (which included amending the Constitution) in 1995. Lesotho and Zimbabwe are the only countries demonstrating current legislative change in their citizenship policies.

ACQUISITION OF CITIZENSHIP

This section describes five significant routes to acquiring citizenship in the countries of SADC: birth, descent, and naturalization, as well as marriage and registration. The acquisition of citizenship by descent is examined in both the first and the second generations. Our research did not cover the acquisition of citizenship through adoption procedures nor through the transfer of territory from one state to another.

In addition to the discussion in the following sections, much of the information is presented in tabular form. Table 2 gives an overview of the two principal routes of acquiring citizenship: birth and descent.[11] Table 3 gives an overview of the conditions that different countries attach to naturalization. Finally, Tables 4 and 5 give an overview of the marriage and the registration routes to citizenship.

The Right to Citizenship by Territorial Birth

As Table 2 shows, the right to citizenship based upon birth in the territory is relatively limited in SADC. This is despite the fact that the legal tradition of many of these countries came from the British Commonwealth where the right of *jus soli* existed.[12] Only four countries formally apply a right to citizenship based upon birth in the territory: Lesotho, Namibia, South Africa, and Zambia.[13] Moreover, the exceptions to this rule are very significant in at least three of these countries: (a) Lesotho only extends this right upon choice of Lesotho citizenship and registration at age 18; (b) South Africa only extends this right to children of at least one permanent resident; and (c) Zambia permits the child of established residents to apply to a Citizenship Board for confirmation of citizenship at age 21. Namibia appears to be the most liberal *jus soli* country. Article 4(1)(d) of its Constitution states that children born in Namibia, one of whose parents is ordinarily resident in the country, shall be citizens by birth if neither parent is a diplomat, a career foreign representative, a member of foreign security service, or an illegal resident.

The Lesotho and Zambian rules are appropriated from the other side—from the French legal tradition that does not have a right to citizenship by virtue of territorial birth. In the case of Mozambique, the first foreign generation born in Mozambique receives citizenship by birth upon declaration either at birth or at the age of 18. The second foreign generation born in the country receives citizenship by birth at birth without declaration. With variations, Lesotho, Mozambique and Zambia thus operate *jus soli* regimes conditional on registration at age of majority.

There are some other exceptions to the SADC absence of the right to *jus soli* that are relatively small. One is for a child who would otherwise be stateless. Such a child enjoys the right to citizenship based on territorial birth in Angola, Lesotho, Seychelles, South Africa, and Zambia (upon application to and confirmation by the Citizenship Board). Another exception is for a child born to unknown parents. Such a child enjoys the right to citizenship based on territorial birth in Lesotho, Namibia, and Zambia (upon application to and confirmation by the Citizenship Board).

The Right to Citizenship by Descent (First Generation)

As Table 2 shows, the right to citizenship of children of citizens is generally accepted throughout SADC. Every country in SADC provides some form of the right to citizenship based on descent. Table 2 is based on the enjoyment of this right where a single parent is a citizen. Nonetheless, there are some important limitations to this right in a number of the SADC countries. These limitations fit into three categories: territory of birth, registration, and parent restrictions.

Six countries vary this right with respect to territory of birth. Lesotho, Namibia, and South Africa recognize the right of *jus sanguinis* but only for birth outside the territory. These countries have this limitation on the right to citizenship by descent because these countries have the right of *jus soli* for in-country birth to citizens. A second set of countries recognizes different rights for births in the country and births outside. These are: Malawi, Mozambique, and Tanzania.

Of these six countries, three of them impose further limitations on the right to citizenship by descent. These further limitations consist of either registration or choice of nationality requirements. Namibia and South Africa require children born abroad of a parent citizen to register in order to claim citizenship. Mozambique does likewise and additionally requires such children to choose between Mozambican and any other nationality the child may have.

Finally, four countries impose limitations on citizen parents' ability to pass on citizenship to their children. In Swaziland and Tanzania, for children born outside the country only, the citizen parent must be the father. In Malawi, only parent citizens of African race may pass citizenship to their children; children born outside Malawi must additionally be born to a native-born parent.

The Right to Citizenship by Descent (Second Generation)

The situation with respect to the right to citizenship of children of citizens at the second generation is usually particularly important for those generations born outside the country of nationality. In the SADC region, there are, in some cases, relatively large populations of citizens of one SADC country residing in another SADC country.

The second generation right to citizenship should be evaluated together with two other provisions of the laws of citizenship. First, the law of naturalization of the country of birth of the second generation is significant. If the country of birth of the second generation will not grant citizenship, it is particularly important to have the right to second-generation citizenship in the country of first-generation origin. Second, the law of registration of citizenship in the country of first-generation origin is also important. In many instances there is no right to second-generation citizenship by descent but if the child of citizens were to come to the country of origin of his or her parent citizens, he or she could obtain citizenship by registration.

Generally, the right of second generations to citizenship demonstrates the same characteristics as *jus sanguinis* as the first generation. If citizenship can be passed by descent to the first generation of children born abroad, then citizenship can be passed to the second generation in the same way. However, Swaziland imposes the additional requirement of registration for those children born abroad.[14]

For the second generation of children born abroad, the situations of Malawi and Mauritius are substantially different from the rest of the SADC region. Neither Malawi nor Mauritius allows for children born abroad of a parent who is a citizen by descent to receive citizenship. The right of citizenship may be passed only to the first generation.

The Right to Citizenship by Naturalization[15]

Table 3 gives an overview of the right to citizenship by naturalization in the SADC region. There are important differences in the regulation of naturalization with respect to renunciation requirements, prior residence requirements, and knowledge of national language, as well as other features.

Most countries of the SADC region require applicants for naturalization to renounce any prior citizenship in order to be eligible for a new citizenship. Most countries have this as a clear requirement in their governing law of citizenship; a couple of countries apparently exercise this requirement in line with a policy against dual citizenship as a matter of ministerial or departmental discretion (Mozambique and Swaziland).[16]

There are different requirements for proof of renunciation. For instance, Malawi specifically enforces the renunciation requirement via a "Declaration of Renunciation of Citizenship of Another Country." Namibia also specifically enforces the requirement of renunciation through a specific form. Proof of renunciation is not as specific in Mozambique. The level of proof required for renunciation is part of the present controversy in Zimbabwe regarding dual citizenship (discussed below).

There are three clear exceptions to the requirement of renunciation at naturalization. Botswana, the Seychelles, and South Africa do not require applicants for naturalization to renounce prior citizenships. Furthermore, Tanzania only requires renunciation where it is legally possible.

All countries require a period of residence before applicants can be eligible for naturalization. These periods range from five to ten years. Perhaps the strictest residence requirements are leveled against applicants for naturalization in Botswana. Such persons need to have been resident for 10 of the 12 years preceding the application, including the 12 months immediately prior to the application and, further, must have lodged a declaration of intention to apply five to six years before the application. Zambia requires ten years of residence. The shortest periods of residence for eligibility for naturalization are found in South Africa (permanent residence for 12 months immediately prior to application plus four of the eight years prior to application, with exceptions possible), Zimbabwe (five years, with exceptions possible), and Lesotho, Mozambique, Namibia, and the Seychelles (five years).

Knowledge of the languages or culture of the naturalizing country is a common but not universal requirement in SADC. Several countries do not have any language requirements: Mozambique, Namibia, and Zimbabwe. Most others allow for English as well as other languages spoken in the naturalizing country. Only Botswana does not grant eligibility for naturalization upon English language ability; a person must speak Setswana or any other tribal community language in order to be naturalized as a citizen of Botswana.[17] In what some might consider a similar requirement to that of language ability (because it demonstrates some familiarity with the character of the national community), some countries require a demonstration of knowledge of the responsibilities of citizenship (Mauritius, Namibia, the Seychelles and South Africa).

There are a number of other more specific requirements for naturalization. Many countries require applicants to take an oath of allegiance or loyalty. Many also require applicants to be of good character. This "good character" requirement is often demonstrated by lack of a criminal record. Some impose a requirement that applicants for naturalization give evidence of an intention to continue to reside in the naturalizing country. Some require that applicants for naturalization be financially solvent. Some countries have a requirement of sponsors' certificates (Malawi, Tanzania). Some use a notice procedure (Botswana, Tanzania).

The Right to Citizenship by Marriage

Almost all SADC countries have separate provisions relating to the acquisition of citizenship by a spouse married to a national, as shown by Table 4. In these separate provisions, the basis for acquisition of citizenship is the status of being married to a citizen. These separate provisions for foreign spouses are uniformly less onerous than the provisions for naturalization. Zambia is the sole exception, using its system of citizenship by registration to regulate the acquisition of citizenship by foreign spouses.

In the acquisition of citizenship, the status of marriage is for the most part accepted as a formal matter. Only one country, Swaziland, restricts the benefits of marriage to a citizen to those persons married to certain citizens. Persons married to Swaziland citizens by registration enjoy no special benefits. In a number of countries, the provisions are available only to women married to male citizens: Malawi, Swaziland, Tanzania, and Zimbabwe.

Some countries demonstrate a concern with the length of the marriage. This concern is intended to distinguish between genuine marriages and marriages of convenience (in other words, marriages designed by at least one of the partners to avoid otherwise applicable citizenship or immigration laws).[18] This concern is evident in Mauritius, Namibia, and South Africa. Mauritius requires four years of spousal living; Namibia and South Africa require two years of married residence.

The most common relaxation of requirements for persons married to citizens by comparison with acquisition of citizenship by naturalization is to either dispense with or to shorten the residence requirement. Botswana reduces its residence and its notification periods by half. In a number of countries, the residence periods are dispensed with entirely: Lesotho, Mozambique, Tanzania, and Zimbabwe. The requirement of renunciation of prior citizenship is not dispensed with.

The Right to Citizenship by Registration

The acquisition of citizenship by registration is a residual or catch-all category that essentially differs country by country.[19] Other than to cater to the acquisition of citizenship by foreign spouses (considered above) and for stateless persons (considered above), citizenship by registration functions in three main categories. (These are used in Table 5.) First, many pre-independence claimants may become citizens by registration. Second, at least for those SADC countries within the British legal tradition, many applicants whose country of origin is within the Commonwealth may apply for citizenship by registration. More generally, registration caters to applicants from preferred countries of origin. Third, citizenship by registration is used for adoption and for the registration of minor children.

The dates of independence have been marked upon the citizenship laws of the SADC region. At least eight of the SADC countries refer to specific dates as part of their citizenship laws. For the most part, these dates are used to separate the pre-independence and post-independence citizenship regimes, both of which are recognized.[20] Even where there are not specific dates identified in the law of citizenship, other laws are the direct results of either independence or the transition from apartheid.[21] In Namibia, the Namibia Citizenship Special Conferment Act 14 of 1991 bestows Namibian citizenship upon certain descendants of persons who left Namibia owing to persecution by the colonial government that was in control before 1915. The Restoration and Extension of South African Citizenship Act 196 of 1993 was part of the post-apartheid regulation and regularization of citizenship in the former homelands of South Africa.[22]

One feature of pre-independence citizenship regimes, at least in countries with a British legal tradition, was those countries' acceptance on comparatively easy terms of (primarily white) applicants for citizenship from other countries of the Commonwealth. Little is left of that tradition.[23] Only three countries give any preference to applicants from Commonwealth countries of origin (Lesotho, Malawi, and Mauritius) and two of these may give, at least in principle, as much recognition to applicants from "certain African states" or other prescribed countries of origin.

Citizenship by registration is a mode of acquisition often used with respect to adoptions and minor children. Separate provisions exist for the acquisition of citizenship by minor children in at least ten of the SADC countries. Separate provisions exist for adoption in at least five countries. In most instances where there is provision for minors but not for adoption, it may be presumed that adoptions are catered to with the provision for minors. However, the South African position with respect to adoption is significantly different. There, adopted children are considered citizens either by birth or by descent.[24]

A number of SADC countries also provide for miscellaneous categories of acquisition of citizenship. The President or the Minister may grant citizenship in special circumstances in Botswana, Malawi, the Seychelles, and Zambia. Honorary citizenship exists by law in Namibia and Zimbabwe. Only Mauritius provides explicitly for acquisition through the incorporation of territory.

CITIZENSHIP POLICY ISSUES

Dual Citizenship

The issue of dual citizenship is one that is increasingly becoming relevant in countries across the globe. The countries of SADC are no exception to this trend. As a general rule, the issue of dual citizenship is explicitly treated in the citizenship laws of most of the SADC countries. There is, however, a variety of approaches to this complex issue.

The countries of SADC are either relatively tolerant of dual citizenship or intolerant (see Table 6). However, there is no natural or scientific method for classifying them as one or the other. In our view, some national requirements for renunciation do not make for a policy of dual citizenship intolerance. In particular, as is evident from the discussions above, it is a common but not universal feature that naturalizing persons need to renounce any prior citizenship. Likewise, persons acquiring citizenship on the basis of marriage to a country national often have a renunciation requirement. These naturalization or marriage renunciation provisions on their own do not signify intolerance for dual citizenship. This is why we have used the terms 'relatively tolerant' and 'relatively intolerant'.

Some cases of dual citizenship are unavoidable. There are a number of ways in which such persons (after renunciation) or persons not acquiring citizenship by naturalization or marriage may end up in a situation of dual citizenship. Either by marriage or by circumstances of birth (both location and citizenship of parents) dual citizenship may result. Even in countries that explicitly prohibit dual citizenship, there is at the very least a tolerance of temporary dual citizenship. For instance, some laws allow for a period of time such as a year while a married spouse chooses which of two citizenships to renounce.

There is at least one clear line that can be drawn. There are some citizenship laws that explicitly prohibit the holding of dual citizenship. In order to classify a country as tolerant or intolerant of dual citizenship, the important policies are thus those that prohibit either the status of dual citizenship or that mandate the loss of citizenship upon most if not all forms of acquisition of another citizenship (e.g., involuntary acquisition and acquisition by marriage). We have not classified as intolerant those countries that prohibit only the voluntary acquisition of dual citizenship. We have also not classified as intolerant those countries that only mandate loss of citizenship unless there is renunciation at the age of majority.

Using this test, we have found the countries of the SADC region to be fairly evenly divided on the relative tolerance of dual citizenship. Five countries either explicitly prohibit dual citizenship or have a rule that mandates loss of citizenship upon even involuntary or marriage-based acquisition of a foreign citizenship: the Democratic Republic of Congo (DRC), Malawi, Mozambique, Namibia, and Zimbabwe.[25] Eight countries have policies that are relatively tolerant: Botswana, Lesotho, Mauritius, South Africa, Seychelles, Swaziland, Tanzania, and Zambia. It should be emphasized that these policies of tolerance are only relative. For instance, all countries with *de jure* policies of relative tolerance of dual citizenship nonetheless have provisions rendering the dual citizenship holder liable to deprivation of citizenship should the holder exercise his or her citizenship rights in a foreign country.

Loss of Citizenship

As shown in Table 7, there is a remarkable uniformity in the policies of SADC countries with respect to loss/deprivation of citizenship.26 In almost all instances, provisions with respect to loss of citizenship apply only to citizens by registration or naturalization. Mozambique and South Africa have more particularized policies regarding deprivation of citizenship.

The rule is that extended absence in a foreign country without notification can result in loss of citizenship. This period varies from five to seven years. For Namibia, it is combined with permanent residence and is only two years. Only South Africa and Mozambique do not have such a provision.

In general, the countries of SADC share a common policy of potential deprivation of citizenship on grounds of military service or disloyalty to the nation. Only South Africa restricts this significantly, by limiting this to dual citizens. Likewise, there is a common SADC policy of deprivation of citizenship on grounds of acquisition by fraud, though South Africa limits this to citizens by naturalization.

There is perhaps most variation around the loss of citizenship on account of a criminal conviction. The limiting factors on this ground of deprivation are the length of sentence (from 12 months to 5 years) and the time elapsed since acquisition of citizenship (from no limit to within five years). Some countries distinguish between crimes committed inside and outside the country. There is no such ground for deprivation in Botswana and Swaziland and it is limited to trafficking-type convictions in Malawi.

Reacquisition of Citizenship

For a variety of reasons, policy on the reacquisition of citizenship (also termed restoration or resumption) is important.[27] The variety of policies in SADC countries is shown in Table 8. Two significant sources of persons applying for reacquisition of citizenship are persons with recent changes in marital status and persons who return to a country of origin for permanent residence after renunciation.[28] These sources are clearly seen in the identification of the revocable grounds of loss of citizenship. In almost all SADC countries with statutory policies on citizenship, at least four countries, the grounds of dual citizenship and renunciation are covered. In the remaining countries (four), all grounds for loss of citizenship are effectively covered.

The policy on reacquisition of citizenship in SADC countries is flexible and facilitative. There are nearly no limits on what class of citizen may apply for reacquisition. Furthermore, as just discussed, the range of revocable grounds for loss of citizenship is quite broad. Namibia even allows for potential reacquisition of citizenship after loss of citizenship on the grounds of a criminal conviction. Zimbabwe is the exception to this policy, not allowing reacquisition if the grounds for loss of citizenship was that of voluntary renunciation. The conditions of reacquisition are generally minimal: usually renunciation and an oath. Zambia is an exception, requiring an application to its Citizenship Board and evidence of lack of knowledge of loss of citizenship on the part of the applicant. Complementing this relatively generous reacquisition policy, Mauritius and Mozambique provide special procedures for the reacquisition of citizenship by married women.

In most of the SADC laws of citizenship (but not all), formal documentary proof of citizenship is identified. Provision is made for a certificate to be issued in cases of doubt in Botswana, Lesotho, Malawi, Mauritius, Namibia, South Africa, Tanzania, Zambia, and Zimbabwe.[29] Namibia and South Africa have an additional provision for issuing certificates of citizenship upon application. Swaziland makes provisions for a Certificate of Nationality, which may be the result of a successful application to the Citizenship Advisory Board. This certificate would apparently include, but also extend beyond, cases of doubt.

Except for the additional Namibian and South African provisions and for the Swaziland one, these certificates of proof of citizenship only apply to cases of doubt. Moreover, all apply primarily to cases where persons are changing their status of citizenship, for instance with naturalization or renunciation. As a percentage of the citizens of the country, these certificate cases are relatively small in number and are concerned with particular individuals. No SADC country reporting uses these certificates in a significant manner at the population level. The more significant policies on documentation are discussed in the chapter on registration and national identification.

The implementing institution for citizenship policy is usually linked closely to the implementing institution for migration policy. In almost all the countries of SADC, the implementing institution for immigration law is the same as that for citizenship law. One of the exceptions is Swaziland, where the King has responsibility for some aspects of citizenship policy that are not within the domain of the Minister charged with immigration law.

CONCLUSION

A recent study of policy trends in managing citizenship concluded that many states were presently examining and reforming their nationality policies.[30] This study identifies three broad policy trends. First, there is a growing salience of dual nationality and other citizenship and nationality reforms. Second, there is increased attention being paid to the changing rights, benefits, and claim-making of foreign residents. Third, there is a growing visibility and influence of multiple levels of governance and participation.

If one takes those areas as indicative, the SADC region fits into at least two of these international trends. The question of dual nationality in particular and citizenship status in general is one that is persistent and not easily solved. This is a policy question that impacts particularly on the population of women and children. In the SADC region, this policy question is one that overlaps with the policy on national identification documentation (addressed in Chapter 2). Already in South Africa and increasingly in other countries, policy-makers are attempting to draw a sharp distinction between full members and others, e.g. between citizens and foreigners. Citizenship is being used more and more as a policy tool in a number of social policy areas such as health services and social security, as well as municipal services. Far from nation-states withering away in this age of globalization, in Southern Africa at least, they are using the marks and symbols of globalization (passports, national identification cards and the like) to good policy effect. As this trend increases, status questions such as the place of dual citizens become increasingly pressing.

Second, the SADC region is also becoming increasingly concerned with the claims-making processes of foreign residents. In addition to wondering about dual citizens, policy-makers are investigating the status of permanent residents and various classes of temporary residents. One aspect of this trend, particularly apparent in the countries of the SADC region, is the notion that citizenship must be understood to be linked with immigration status. While patriotic feelings are high, there is, at the same time, recognition that some persons use citizenship as a way of staking a claim (to work or to residence) that is more closely related to immigration concerns than to citizenship policy. The point is that there is a greater awareness of the material benefits of citizenship and an acceptance of the multiplicity of motives for claiming citizenship. Even if the claims of foreign residents are dismissed, they are increasingly being at least considered within some kind of legal process.

However, there is as yet relatively little real impact of multiple sites of nationality in the SADC region. Neither SADC nor the African Union (AU) is close to being in a position to usurp or really even influence the citizenship regime of a nation-state as a source of national membership policy. It is economics not politics that is driving or will drive change in citizenship policies in SADC.

2 POPULATION REGISTRATION AND IDENTIFICATION

INTRODUCTION

Population registration and identification refers to documenting and keeping specified records of persons within a given country and issuing identification documents to persons so registered. The primary objective of registration is to enable a state to identify persons found in its territory as well as their socio-economic status. Population registration and identification also plays a direct role in the immigration regime in that it enables citizens and non-citizens to be known, thus facilitating the enforcement of immigration laws. By facilitating the identification of persons, registration and identification enables a country to secure its borders and protect the exclusive rights of citizens without prejudicing non-citizens working, visiting, trading or receiving asylum in the country.

Registration and identification of persons has become even more important in a modern, globalised world characterised by increased mobility of the factors of production including capital, goods, services and persons. Insofar as it facilitates the identification and tracing of persons, registration and identification makes it easy for individuals to access a wide range of benefits and services. This is because should they default, they can be traced and made accountable for their actions and transactions. Related to this, registration and identification of persons makes it easier to deal with the negative aspects of globalisation such as international terrorism, human trafficking and trade in drugs.

This chapter reviews the laws relating to population registration and identification in the SADC region. As with the previous chapter, the focus is on aspects that are relevant to immigration regulation, namely: the requirement to register; content of the registers and their relevance to migration; and the reliability of the documents issued pursuant to registration.

The principal acts of legislation that will be examined are: Botswana's *National Registration Act*[31]; *Malawi's Aliens (Registration and Status) Act*[32]; Lesotho's *Passport Services and National Identity Cards Services Act* of 1984[33] and the *Mozambican Identification Decree* of 1999.[34] Others include Namibia's *Identification Act* of 1996[35]; South Africa's *Identification Act* of 1997;[36] Swaziland's *Identification Order* of 1998;[37] Tanzania's *Registration and Identification of Persons Act* of 1986;[38] Zambia's *National Registration Act*[39] and Zimbabwe's *National Registration Act* of 1976.[40] Of these laws, the Tanzanian Act is not yet in operation but it will be dealt with as if it were in force.

REGISTRATION OF POPULATION

Some laws in the SADC deal with registration and identification separately while others cover the two under one statute.[41] However, the basic provisions relating to registration are essentially similar. The statutes make provisions as to the requirement to register; registration procedures; particulars to be included in the register; the evidential value of the particulars in registries; changes in particulars relating to registered persons; and offences and penalties.

Requirement to Register

In all jurisdictions where the requirement to register exists, it applies to citizens and/or persons who are lawfully and permanently resident in a particular country.[42] The majority of countries make the registration of persons mandatory and impose the obligation on individuals to register themselves or on specified officers to maintain population registers. In Botswana, every citizen aged 16 years or older must apply for registration within one month of reaching the age of 16 years or, if they became a citizen of Botswana after reaching the age of 16, within one month of so doing.[43] Similarly, in Zimbabwe, any person who is resident in an area which has been designated for registration, or who becomes resident in such an area must, unless already registered, apply for registration within a month of qualifying to do so.[44] This duty is a continuing one and cannot be deemed to have been extinguished by reason only of the fact that a resident has failed to register within the prescribed period. A "resident" is defined as an inhabitant of Zimbabwe who has resided therein for a continuous period of not less than six months and has attained the prescribed age and is not a member of such class of persons as is prescribed. In Zambia, where an area has been declared to be covered by the National Registration Act, every resident of such an area must attend before the Registrar and register themselves within fourteen days.[46]

In South Africa, Namibia and Swaziland, the responsibility to compile and maintain the population register has been imposed on specified government officials. This may suggest that, although registration of persons is compulsory, the responsibility to ensure that it happens lies primarily with the government rather than the individuals themselves. However, as we shall see below, at the end of the day, whether or not registration is compulsory depends on the functions that the law assigns to registration.

In some jurisdictions, registration does not appear to be compulsory for certain categories of persons. For example, although the title of Section 7 of the Arrangement of Sections part of the Tanzanian Act, reads "compulsory registration of persons," the section does not actually make registration compulsory. The material part of the Section reads, "every person of or above the age of eighteen years who, on or after the commencement of this Act, is or resides in the United Republic and to whom this Act applies *may make an application for registration...*". Section 7(2) empowers the Minister, where he or she deems necessary in the interest of administrative or other convenience, to order the progressive registration of persons who are resident in the areas that may be specified. Even where the Minister has made such an order, persons affected by it *"may apply for registration."* However, Section 8(3) provides that, "Every alien who is subject to this Act shall apply for registration." The totality of these provisions is such that in Tanzania no person other than an alien is obliged to register.

In Malawi, only "aliens" are required to register.[47] There is no law that provides for general registration of the population. However, such legislation is under consideration.

In Zimbabwe, registration is not compulsory as such. However, possession of a registration number is a requirement for so many things that no one can afford to be without one. The registration number is required for, among other things, registering children at school. For this reason, many children, mostly in rural areas who were not registered at birth, do so at the time of joining schools. The national registration number is also required for social security, opening bank accounts, and obtaining a driving licence and passport. The registration number also functions as the voter's registration number.

Registration Authorities

The responsibility relating to registration is placed on specified public offices. In South Africa, the responsibility to compile and maintain the population register has been imposed on the Director-General of Home Affairs.[48] In Swaziland and Zimbabwe these powers are vested in the Registrar-General.[49] The Chief Registration Officer discharges the same functions in Malawi and Zambia.[50] Under the Namibian Act, the responsibility of registering persons is directly vested in the Minister of Home Affairs.[51] In Botswana and Tanzania, the powers to issue and regulate identity documents are vested in the Registrar of National Registration appointed by the relevant Minister.[52] In Lesotho, the system of registration is linked in the system of issuing identity documents, a function which is vested in "appropriate government offices in all towns as well as in the prescribed offices of chiefs in the villages." [53]

Certain functions of the registrars may be discharged by their assistants duly appointed under the relevant law. In Botswana and Tanzania, the relevant Minister may appoint assistant registrars and other public officials to assist the registrars in the discharge of their duties.[54] In Botswana, Swaziland, South Africa and Namibia, the laws empower the Registrar-General, Director-General and the Minister, respectively, to delegate most of their powers vested in them under the law.[55] In Zimbabwe, the day-to-day functions of registration of persons are discharged by the Chief Procurement Officer, National Registration, Voters and Electoral Issues and their staff.

Registration Procedures

There are two main procedures for registration. The first is application by the person to whom the registration provisions pertain. This procedure is followed in Botswana where, as mentioned above, the law requires persons to apply for registration within one month of obtaining qualifications to do so. Under the Tanzanian and Zambian Acts, a person seeking or liable to register must make an application to the registrar in such manner and on such form as may be prescribed.[56] In Zambia, this involves permitting one's photograph to be taken by the registrar and filling out the application for registration form (Form 1).

In Malawi, the procedure for registration of "aliens" is subsumed in the procedure for obtaining identity cards. Section 5 of the Aliens (Registration and Status) Act requires "aliens" to apply for identity cards. Such applications are made to registration officers who, in turn, transmit the same to the Chief Registration Officer who, if satisfied that the applicant has entered Malawi lawfully and is entitled to remain therein, issues such applicant an identity card. By the same token, the applicant is registered. In Lesotho, where the procedures of registration and obtaining identity cards are also linked, an applicant for an identity card or a card other than a national identity card can obtain it in their district of domicile, their place of employment or at places prescribed by the Minister.[57]

The second main procedure for registration is by way of information for the population register being compiled by a specified public official from any appropriate source. Thus, the South African Identification Act permits the Director-General, in compiling and maintaining the population register, to utilise any information contained in the population register which existed immediately prior to the commencement of the Act, as well as the information contained in any document kept by the Director-General under any law, as appropriate.[58] The Namibian Identification Act and the Swazi Order provide that the particulars for the compilation and maintenance of the population register shall be obtained from the documents that may be available to the Minister and Registrar respectively.[59] In Zimbabwe, the population register is compiled from information contained in various registers maintained on a centralised and computerised database maintained in the Registrar-General's office. Also, the office of the Registrar-General runs mobile registration services to reach out to people in rural areas who, for cost reasons, are not able to come to town to register.

Particulars to be Included in the Register

The particulars to be included in the register which are common to most laws are: national identity number where applicable, full name, residential address, sex, date of birth, place of birth, occupation, postal address, marital status, full/maiden name of spouse and other particulars relating to marital status. The laws of Botswana and South Africa expressly require the particulars of marriage contained in the marital register or other documents relating to the contracting of marriage.

Other common particulars to be furnished for the purposes of registration are: distinguishing features, colour of eyes, nationality at birth, proof of birth, citizenship certification number, village/town, ward/house number, names of parents, parents' nationalities and whether they are still living. In addition, applicants for registration must supply a photograph, palm prints and/or fingerprints.[60]

Other requirements which are not common to all legislation are the particulars of tribal affiliation and registration and liability for national service[61] and, in the case of non-citizens: passport number, work permit number, and residence/exempt permit number.[62]

The laws of Namibia, South Africa, and Swaziland appear to empower the registration authorities to include in the population register particulars of persons who are dead or who have departed the country. If a person is dead, the entry should constitute the particulars furnished when notice of his or her death was given. If he or she has permanently departed from the country, the entry should consist of the date of departure and particulars concerning the cancellation in the prescribed manner of the identity document.[63]

In South Africa, the Director-General is required to assign an identity number to every person whose particulars have been included in the population register. The identity number must be compiled in the prescribed form and must include the date of birth and gender, and whether or not the person is a South African citizen. No other particulars whatsoever of the person can be included.[64] An identical provision is found under Section 5 of the Swazi Order.

Verification of Particulars

The statutes of South Africa, Namibia, Swaziland and Zambia empower the registration authorities to request any person to furnish proof of the correctness of any particulars that have been furnished with respect to said person in any documents for the purposes of registration. The authorities may also investigate or cause to be investigated any matter with respect to which particulars are required to be recorded in the population registers.[65] The Tanzanian and Malawi Acts are silent on this matter.

Evidential Value of the Particulars in Registries

The statutes do not generally allude to the evidential value of the contents of registers except in relation to the probative value of certificates produced and issued on the basis of the contents of registers. However some laws do address this matter generally or in specified situations. Under the Registration Acts of Botswana, Namibia, Tanzania and Zambia, any document signed by the registration authority certifying a copy or extract of any record by the registrar is, in any criminal proceedings under those Acts, *prima facie* evidence of the facts stated therein.[66]

An interesting position is found in the Tanzanian Act. According to Section 17, "the burden of proving the truth of the contents of any application for registration under this act shall be on the applicant, or any other person alleging the truth of those contents." As will be seen below, the evidential value of these contents does not seem to change even after they have been included in the register.

IDENTIFICATION

The principal way by which the identity of persons is ascertained is by production of identification documents specifically designed for that purpose or any other secondary documents acceptable to serve for that purpose. In SADC countries, the primary means of identification is an "Identity Document" or "Identity Card" which is issued after prescribed procedures have been exhausted. In some countries, the other documents that are acceptable include passports and drivers licences.

Requirement to Hold Identity Cards

The requirement to hold identity cards is provided for either directly or indirectly under the laws of countries where laws on population registration and identification exist. Under the laws of Lesotho and South Africa, every citizen and permanent resident who has attained the age of 16 or over must apply for an identity card.[67] Under the Botswana, Tanzanian and Zambian Acts, once a person has registered, he or she must be issued with an identity card.[68]

Under the legislation of Namibia and Swaziland registration does not automatically lead to issuance of, or requirement to hold, identity documents. Such documents are issued separately upon an application being made to the relevant registration officer. However, both laws provide that application for identity documents "shall be made within such period as may be prescribed in respect of any category of person."[69] This indicates that the power to require some persons to apply for identity cards is reserved.

Either way, even where it is not compulsory to possess an identity document, persons may be compelled to apply for the same depending on the uses for which the identity documents may be required. As will be seen, in some countries, production of identity documents is required to access so many services, in both the public and private sectors, that every eligible person applies for one whether or not strictly required to do so by registration and identification laws.

Authorities who Issue Identity Documents

In Botswana and Tanzania, the power to issue and regulate identity documents is vested in the Registrar of National Registration appointed by the relevant Minister.[70] The Zambian Act allows any registrar working under the auspices of the Registrar-General to issue identity documents that are known as national registration cards. In Swaziland and Zimbabwe these powers are vested in the Registrar-General.[71] The Director-General and the Minister of Home Affairs discharge the same functions in South Africa and Namibia respectively.[72] All legislation allows the appointment of assistants and delegation of the function of issuing identity documents.[73] For example, in Zimbabwe, the day-to-day functions of registration of persons are discharged by the Procurement Officer, National Registration, Voters and Electoral Issued and their staff. As seen above, in Lesotho, national identity documents are issued in districts of domicile, places of employment and any other place prescribed by the Minister.

Requirements for Obtaining Identity Documents

The first and foremost requirement for obtaining identity documents is that a person be eligible to register under the relevant law and has so registered.[74] That is to say, a person must be a citizen or a resident of a particular country. Under the Namibian, South African, Swazi and Zambian Acts, identity documents are issued to persons who have attained the age of 16.[75] The same applies in Zimbabwe although this is not expressly provided for in the principal legislation. Applicants for identity documents are required to supply photographs as well as fingerprints.[76]

Procedures for Issuing Identity Documents

The statutory procedures for issuance of identity documents differ slightly from country to country. Under the laws of Botswana and Tanzania, every person who has been registered must be issued an identity card immediately after registration; in the case of Tanzania, after paying the prescribed fees.[77] In Namibia, South Africa and Swaziland, identity documents are issued upon making an application to the prescribed officer.[78] And, under Section 6(2) of the Namibian Identification Act, a proof of registration is, for the purposes of the Act, proof that the person concerned has applied for an identity card. According to the laws of Namibia and South Africa, if it comes to the attention of an officer acting in the service of the Ministry of Home Affairs that a person who meets the criteria for applying for the identity documents has not done so, that officer must take such steps as may be necessary to ensure that that person applies for an identity card.[79] What this means is that both the individual as well as the government can initiate the process of obtaining identity documents.

In Zimbabwe, if a registration officer is satisfied as to the identity of an applicant for registration and the accuracy of any information given in connection with the application for registration, the office must issue a notice in writing indicating the date on which the applicant applied for registration and the place at which, and time when, they may receive their identity document. When an applicant for registration surrenders to the registration officer the notice issued as explained above, at the place and within the period specified in that notice, the registration officer must, if satisfied of the identity of the applicant, issue an identity document.[80]

Contents of Identity Documents

Some statutes expressly specify the particulars that must be contained in the identity documents[81] while others simply confer upon the relevant Minister the power to determine what the content of identity documents should be.[82] The common contents of identity documents are: identity number; full name; date and place of birth; citizenship status; photograph of the person concerned and fingerprints. Others are colour of eyes, height of the person concerned, the region of origin and the place of application for registration.

Relationship between Identity Documents and Migration Status

As noted above, the contents of an identity document do include the nationality of the holder. However, this does not mean that identity documents are necessarily conclusive proof of migration status, or indeed, of any other of their contents. The probative value given to identity cards differs from one country to another.

Under Article 2 of the Mozambican Identification Act, an identity document issued under the Act is sufficient proof of the identity of its possessor.[83] The identity document does not mention the nationality of the holder. However, it does include, among other things, the names of the ascendants of the bearer and the place and date of their birth. Therefore, to the extent that these details are proof of nationality under the citizenship laws, they are also proof of immigration status.

According to Section 12 of the Botswana Act, "the identity card shall be *prima facie* proof of the particulars stated therein." Under the National Registration Regulations of 12 June 1987, the identity card in Botswana includes all the particulars mentioned in the foregoing section including nationality of the holder.[84] This means that, in Botswana, an identity card is *prima facie* proof of the nationality stated therein.

Under Regulations 3 and 4 of the Zambian National Registration Regulations, a national registration card must bear a different colour depending on whether a person is a citizen of Zambia, the Commonwealth or an "alien". Zambian citizens must be issued green cards while Commonwealth citizens and "aliens" must be given pink and blue cards, respectively. By the ordinary rules of evidence, the bearer of a card with a particular colour is presumed to be a national of a country to which a card with such a colour can be issued. However, in practice, this presumption is not conclusive.

Many other statutes accord the identity documents the status of proof of identity without expressly specifying their probative value as to the contents of those documents including with respect to nationality.[85] However, in practice, an identity document issued after the procedure of registration is taken as evidence of what it states including the nationality of the holder. For example in Zimbabwe, the production of an identity document or the identity number for persons under 16 years of age, is a *sine qua non*, as well as sufficient proof, for access to services reserved for citizens such as free or subsidised education, health care and social welfare.

In South Africa, immigration enforcement agencies routinely ask for identity cards in operations designed to identify and deport illegal immigrants. Production of a South African ID is taken to be proof of South African citizenship unless the validity of the ID is doubted or rejected for mischievous reasons.[86] By the same token, if an identity document states that a person is not a citizen, such a person will be taken not to be a citizen.

This is in sharp contrast to the Tanzanian Act. According to Section 10 of the Act, there are two types of identity documents that will be issued: one for citizens of the United Republic and another one for "aliens" resident in the United Republic. However, according to Section 17, which in the marginal note is tellingly titled "no presumption of truth of contents of identity cards," "the burden of proving the truth of the contents of...an identity card issued under this act shall be on...the holder of the identity card, or any other person alleging the truth of those contents." This means that in Tanzania, an identity card will not, in legal and strict terms, constitute even *prima facie* evidence of anything it contains, including nationality/citizenship.

Relationship to Travel Documents

To the extent to which an identity document is proof of immigration status, it is *ipso facto* also proof as to whether a person is entitled to travel documents and, if so, which ones. Thus, if a person is a citizen, he or she will be entitled to at least an ordinary passport issued to citizens and vice versa. It is for this reason that one of the details required on the application forms for passports is the national identification number. In Zimbabwe, this is the first item number to be filled in on the form.

The identity documents may also serve as proof of the authenticity of travel documents. This is because, while the serial number as well as other contents of travel documents can change, the identity number of the holder cannot.

Because they are obtained after producing identity documents, travel documents are acceptable in many countries as alternative or secondary means of identification. For example, a person required to identify themselves in terms of Section 17(1) of the South African Identification Act may do so by producing an identity card or "any other proof of identity issued by the State on which the name and photograph of the holder appear."[87] This would include a passport. Under Section 10(b) of the Namibian Identification Act, passports and other travel documents are prescribed as proof of identity of equal probative value to the identity document. Under Section 32 of Zimbabwe's Public Order and Security Act,[88] "identity document" includes identity documents issued under Section 7 of the National Registration Act as well as a passport or a driver's licence issued by the Government of Zimbabwe or a foreign government.

Period of Validity of Identity Documents

Under Section 9 of the Botswana Act, as amended by the National Registration (Amendment) Act of 1993, an identity card is valid for 10 years and is renewable for further periods of 10 years for as long as the holder of the card qualifies for registration under the Act. However, when the applicant is under 21 years of age, and possesses dual citizenship in accordance with the Citizenship Act, his or her identity card is valid only until he or she reaches the age of 21 years, and can only be renewed if he or she then assumes Botswana citizenship. For a non-citizen, the duration of validity of his or her identity card is coterminous with the period for which the non-citizen is entitled to remain in Botswana.

In Zimbabwe, the identity document lasts forever. Even the material used in making the cards is meant to ensure that they last for a long time. While the National Registration Act makes provisions for correction of errors, alteration of particulars and replacement of identity documents, these provisions are not easily resorted to. For example, change of appearance is not a good enough reason to seek to change the photograph on the identity document. The Zambian Act also does not prescribe the period of validity of the national registration card. However, it allows for replacement if the card ceases to accurately represent the identity of the holder in any material particular.[89] The Laws of South Africa, Tanzania, Swaziland and Namibia are silent on this aspect.

Production of Identity Documents on Demand

A number of laws make provisions requiring the production of identity documents when so required by competent officers. Under Sections 10(1) and 17(1) of the Namibian and South African Identification Acts, respectively, an authorised officer may at any time request any person reasonably presumed to have attained the age of 16 years to prove his or her identity to that officer by the production of his or her identity card. In Namibia, the person so required to produce an identity document may produce his or her passport or any other proof of identity issued by the state on which the name and photograph of the holder appear.[90] Under Section 18 of the Lesotho Act, national identity cards or identity cards other than national identity cards must be produced to police officers or other authorised persons on demand.

Identity documents are required not only for identification purposes, but also as a precondition for receiving certain services provided by the State. Thus, under Section 14(1) of the Tanzanian Act, the Minister responsible for matters relating to citizenship is empowered, after consultations with relevant authorities, to specify situations, services, facilities or other things, the granting or obtaining of which may be provided depending on the condition that a person identifies themself by the name and number on their identity card. Section 14(3) expressly empowers any immigration officer, in the lawful discharge of their duties, to require any person purporting to have registered under the Act, to produce an identity card for inspection.

Under section 10 of the Zambian Act, the Minister may empower any authority to request any person who is applying for the grant of any licence, permit or other document, to produce their national registration card for inspection before the services required are rendered. Among the authorities that have been so empowered are all municipal councils, town councils and rural councils. The same section also empowers the Chief Registrar and any registrar to demand the production of identity documents.

In Zimbabwe, the identity document is required for some 23 services and facilities including registration at school, voting, and opening bank accounts. In addition, under Section 32(2) of the Public Order and Security Act of 2002, every person of or over the age of 16 years must, when in a public place, carry an identity document. Section 32(3) specifies other situations in which a person may be required by a police officer to produce an identity document including at police roadblocks, at public gatherings or public meetings of a political nature and during the investigation or prevention of crime. The police are empowered to detain a person until such time as his or her identity is established or verified to their satisfaction.

CONCLUSION

Population registration and identification can play a role in immigration regimes because the easier it is to identify and trace persons, the easier it becomes for countries to regulate migration. As far as the relevant laws in SADC countries are concerned, the first notable feature is that some countries have not enacted such laws. One country has enacted such a law but it is not in force.

Where such laws have been enacted there are, as with birth and death registration legislation, marked differences in the substance of the laws as well as administrative arrangements for their implementation. For example, registration of persons is compulsory under some laws and voluntary under others. In some countries the system of registration is based on compilation of data by public officials while under other laws it is based on application by the persons wishing to register.

The contents of population registers and identity documents do not possess equal evidential value in all countries. Under some laws they are *prima facie* evidence of the particulars contained therein. Under other legislation, such registers and documents do not have any evidential value apart, probably, from being admissible as evidence.

The systems of administration of registration and documentation differ markedly. In some countries, all registers are centralized and integrated under one office. In others, different ministries maintain various registries with little co-ordination.

Chapter 3 REGISTRATION OF BIRTHS AND DEATHS

INTRODUCTION

An important aspect of a population regime is the registration of births, marriages and deaths occurring in a jurisdiction, as well as those taking place abroad involving citizens or permanent residents of a particular country. Registration of births, marriages and deaths serves several functions including ascertaining the inhabitants' civil status, collection of statistical data and monitoring demographic trends and their causes. For example, in Tanzania, the Registrar-General is not only supposed to compile annually the summary of births and deaths, they are also required to "report on the increase or decrease of the population of the country, and on any special causes appearing to affect the same."[91] When this law was first enacted, immigration was one of the significant causes of population increase. The registration of deaths also enables the authorities to know the cause of death and, if it was unnatural, to take the requisite legal steps.

The registration of births and deaths plays an important role in immigration control. Most of the details that are recorded at birth such as date, place of birth and parentage are very crucial to issues of citizenship and identification. They, in turn, are critical to movement-related rights such as the right to enter, remain in and leave a country. In other words, the registration of births creates the first primary evidence as to the immigration status of the inhabitants of a country.

The registration of deaths enables the authorities to be aware of the passing away of the persons concerned. This facilitates the enforcement of the provisions of registration and identification laws that require identity documents of deceased persons to be surrendered. In turn, this prevents the misuse and abuse of the identity documents of deceased persons to gain movement-related rights by persons who would otherwise not be entitled to such rights.

This chapter sketches and compares laws relating to registration of births, marriages and deaths in SADC countries, focussing on those aspects of the laws that are relevant to immigration. The principal acts of legislation discussed here are:

- Botswana's *Births and Deaths Registration Act* (the Botswana Act)[92]

- Malawi's *Births and Deaths Registration Act* (the Malawi Act)[93]

- Mauritius' *Civil Status Act* (the Mauritius Act)[94]

- South Africa's *Births and Deaths Registration Act* (the South African Act)[95]

- Swaziland's *Births, Marriages and Deaths Registration Act* (the Swazi Act)[96]

- Tanzania's *Births and Deaths Registration Ordinance* (the Tanzania Ordinance)[97]

- Zambia's *Births and Deaths Registration Act* (the Zambian Act)[98] and

- Zimbabwe's *Births and Deaths Registration Act* (the Zimbabwe Act).[99] Where available, the accompanying regulations and rules are also analysed.

REGISTRATION OF BIRTHS

Registrars and Registries of Births

In Malawi, Tanzania, Zambia and Zimbabwe, the duty of maintaining registries of births and deaths is assigned to the Registrar-General.[100] In Botswana and Swaziland, this function is vested in the Registrar of Births and Deaths[101] while in Mauritius and South Africa, the same duty rests with the Registrar of Civil Status and the Director-General, respectively.[102] The laws allow the day-to-day discharge of the functions of the principal registration officer to be carried out by assistants, as well as District Registrars operating at district level. In the case of Mauritius, the equivalent of the District Registry is known as the Civil Status Sub-Office.

Duty to Register Births

In some countries, registration of births is compulsory for everyone. In others, registration of births is not compulsory except for prescribed persons or in designated geographic areas. The countries in which registration of all births is compulsory are Mauritius, South Africa, Swaziland, Zambia and Zimbabwe.[103] Botswana's Act makes provisions for both voluntary registration and compulsory registration. The latter provisions apply in districts or areas specified by the Minister in the schedule while the former provisions apply in districts or areas which have not been so specified.[104] Under Malawi's Act and Tanzania's Ordinance, the registration of a birth of a child is compulsory only if one or both parents are of European, American or Asiatic race or origin. In Tanzania, this includes a Somali.[105] Identical sections 18(3) and 27 of the Malawi and Tanzanian legislation respectively empower government to extend compulsory registration of births and deaths to all persons of any particular race, class, tribe, or other group or to all or some inhabitants of any particular town, district or other area.

It is noteworthy that the imposition of compulsory registration requirements on persons of certain races only is found in legislation that is fairly old and applies to persons who are not indigenous. These are the same persons who, during the colonial period, had their entry into and residence in the relevant countries controlled or restricted. This establishes a link between laws relating to registration of births and deaths on one hand and the immigration regimes on the other. Whatever may have been the justification of such laws at the time they were introduced, the constitutional validity of laws that impose duties on individuals on the basis of race or tribe is now highly questionable.

The Content of Birth Registers

The laws require separate registers of births to be maintained in which prescribed details are recorded. These details, as well as the form in which they are to be presented, are normally provided for in regulations or rules made under the principal legislation. The most common details that must be entered in the register are: the serial number of registration; the date and place of birth; the sex and full name of the child; full name, address and nationality of father; name, address and qualification/description of the informant; date of registration and signature of the registering officer.[106]

There are some additional details that are required under the laws of some countries but not under those of the others. Thus, under the Zimbabwean law, in addition to the above, an entry in the Birth Register must also include the identity number of the person being registered that is assigned at birth as well as the national identity card numbers of both parents. In addition, the register must include the birth number of the person being registered. Under Tanzania's law, the register must include the baptismal name if added or altered after registra-

tion of birth. In Zambia, the Zambia National Provident Fund (Z.N.P.F) or any other social security scheme number of both parents, if any, must be indicated.

Mode of Birth Registration

There are various procedures prescribed for children born in different circumstances. First and foremost, the laws specify which persons must report the birth of a child, if such child is subject to compulsory registration. The right or the duty (where registration is compulsory) to register the birth of a child born alive is primarily imposed on its father or mother. In the absence or inability of the father or mother, any person present at the birth including medical personnel, an occupier of dwellings where a child was born or any person having charge of the child, must give notice of birth to the registrar or any other prescribed officer.[107] Any such officer must then report the birth to the registrar.

In the case of Mauritius, when a birth takes place on board any ship or aircraft registered in Mauritius, the master of the ship or aircraft must draw up a memorandum of the birth. On the arrival of the ship in any harbour of Mauritius or the landing of the aircraft in Mauritius, the master must deliver the memorandum to the Director of Shipping or the Director of Civil Aviation, as the case may be, who must transmit it to the Registrar of Civil Status for registration in the appropriate register.[108]

The notice of birth must be given in the prescribed form and within the prescribed time. In Botswana, Malawi and Tanzania, notice of birth must be given within three months. Under Swazi and Zimbabwean law, the period within which notice of a birth must be given is sixty days and forty-two days, respectively. In South Africa and Zambia this period is set at 30 days while in Mauritius it is 45 days.[109] A more or less similar procedure applies in the case of stillbirth. However, in Zimbabwe, notice of a stillbirth must be given within five days.[110]

If a birth has not been registered within twelve months, it can only be registered with the permission of the prescribed officer, usually the highest registration authority. In Malawi, Swaziland, Tanzania, Zambia and Zimbabwe permission for late registration must be obtained from the Registrar-General. In Tanzania and Zimbabwe, such authority is required only if the birth has not been reported within ten years and one year respectively. In Botswana and South Africa, application for late registration must be made to the District Registrar and the Director-General respectively.[111] Under the law of Mauritius, a birth that has not been registered within the prescribed time cannot be registered except upon an order of a District Magistrate.[112]

Before permission for late registration is given, the authorities will take such steps as are necessary to verify the birth and the reasons for late registration. For example, in South Africa, the Director-General may demand that reasons for late registration be furnished and that fingerprints be taken of the person whose notice of birth is given. In Tanzania, a person seeking to register the birth of a child who is ten years or over must, among other things, first obtain a certificate of proof of citizenship of the parents of the child from the District Immigration Officer, and the father or the mother and the child for whom registration is sought must attend a hearing before the District Registration Officer.[113]

All legislation makes provision for children born out of wedlock who, under some legislation are referred to as "illegitimate children." Under the laws of Malawi, Tanzania and Zimbabwe no person is required to give information acknowledging that he is the father of such a child.[114] Under Swazi and Zambian laws, a person who is the father of a child born out of wedlock is not even required, as a father, to give notice of birth of such a child.[115] All legislation prohibits entering the name of any person as the father of any child born out of wedlock in a birth information form or any register except at the joint request of the mother and the person who, in the presence of the registration officer, acknowledges to be the father of the child in the form and manner prescribed.[116]

The requirement for a separate procedure for registration of children born of unmarried couples is intended to avoid creating paternity disputes which, in some jurisdictions, have occurred. As such it may be understandable. However, the relevant provisions are laden with prejudice and stigma which may no longer be warranted. For example, the reference to children born out of wedlock as "illegitimate" in the Botswana, Malawi, Tanzanian, Zambian and Zimbabwean legislation is probably no longer acceptable. The term "child born out of wedlock" used in the Swazi and South African Acts is more appropriate.

The laws also make provision for the registration of newborn foundlings who are referred to as "exposed child" under the laws of Malawi and Tanzania; "abandoned child" in South Africa, Zambia and Zimbabwe; and simply as "a new born [sic] who has been found" under the Mauritius Act. In Malawi, Tanzania, Zambia and Zimbabwe, any person who finds such a child, as well as any person in whose charge such a child may be placed, must give such information as the informant possesses for the purposes of registering its birth.[117] In South Africa, the social worker or an authorised officer must give notice of birth of an abandoned child after an inquiry with respect to whether the child concerned has been conducted in terms of the Child Care Act of 1983.[118] In Mauritius, such notice must be given to the police, who, after taking forensic evidence, must prepare and send a report to the Permanent Secretary, Ministry of Social Security, who in turn will take all the necessary steps to declare the birth of the child and arrange for its care.

Under Section 16 of the Zimbabwe Act, when notice of birth of any person is given under the Act, but at the time of giving such notice the place or date of such birth or both are not known, the Registrar-General may, after due inquiry, direct the registration of such birth notwithstanding the lack of such information and assign to such child a putative place or date of birth, or both.

In Swaziland and Zimbabwe, when an order has been made under any law for the adoption of a child born outside the country, the Registrar-General (Zimbabwe) and the Registrar (Swaziland) must, on application of the adoptive parent, cause the birth of the child to be registered after the adopter has produced the order of adoption or a certified copy thereof, the birth or baptismal certificate of the child or such other documentary evidence which he or she considers to be sufficient and has filled in and signed the prescribed form, adapted as necessary.[119] In Zimbabwe, there must be proof that the adopter, or, in the case of a joint adoption, the male adopter, was a citizen of Zimbabwe at the date of the order of adoption.[120]

Name Changes and Other Particulars in the Birth Registers

The laws allow registered names to be changed in specified circumstances and upon application by specified persons. The typical circumstances under which application to change a name can be made are when the child was registered before it had received a name or when the name by which it was registered has been lawfully altered.[121]

In Zimbabwe, an application to change the name of a child can only be made by "the responsible parent" who is defined as the father of the child. The mother of the child becomes "the responsible parent" only if the father is dead or the mother has been given custody of the child by virtue of a law relating to guardianship of children or if the child is illegitimate. The gender bias in this provision is obvious.

In Malawi, Zambia and Tanzania, application to change the name of the child must be made within two years of the birth being registered. Under the Zimbabwe Act, parents can, at any time before the child has attained the age of 18, make such application. Botswana and Swaziland allow such applications to be made by parents until the child has attained the age of 21. Thereafter, the person who wishes to have their name changed must make the application for alteration of the name.

Before allowing the change of name in the register, the registration officers are empowered to demand such evidence as they may deem necessary. Under Section

18(3) of the Zimbabwe Act, the Registrar-General must, before recording the change, require the execution of a notarial deed setting forth the changes and registering the same in the Deed Registry and advertising the change of name in the government *Gazette*. This requirement may be waived if the Registrar-General is satisfied that the change of name is for a lawful purpose, that the change is not being made for purposes of fraudulent misrepresentation and, in the case of an application to change the name of a person under 18 years, that the responsible parent or legal guardian is competent to make such an application. The laws of Botswana and Zimbabwe require the registrars to make alterations in the birth register without erasing the original name(s) being changed.

Under the laws of Botswana, South Africa, Swaziland and Zimbabwe, when the parents of a child born out of wedlock (and the birth is registered as such) eventually marry, the register can be amended and the birth recorded as it would have been if the parents had been married at the time of the birth.[122] In Zambia, re-registration of a 'legitimated' child must be done in accordance with the provisions of the Legitimacy Act (Cap 52) and within three months of the date of the parents' marriage.[123]

No other alterations in the birth registers are allowed except those intended to correct errors. A typical enabling provision is section 8 of the Zimbabwe Act, which empowers the Registrar-General to direct the corrections of any error in any register, whether it is clerical error or an error of fact or substance. However, such corrections must be made without erasing the original entry and have to be authenticated by the signature of the Registrar-General or Registrar. Identical provisions are found under the laws of Malawi, Tanzania and Zambia.[124]

Under the Botswana Act, the Registrar cannot alter any errors in the registers of birth and death other than those of spelling and transcription unless authorised or directed by an order of the High Court to do so. Therefore, a person who wishes changes of fact or substance made in the register must make an application to the High Court and prove to its satisfaction the material facts in connection with which the application is made.[125]

REGISTRATION OF DEATHS

Death Registries and Registrars

Death registers are maintained at two main levels. The first is the district level where a death register is maintained by a district registrar, who is required to enter therein every death occurring within the district whose particulars have been

reported.[126] In Mauritius, this level is known as a Civil Status Sub-Office where a Civil Status Officer maintains a death register. The second is the national level where the national death register is maintained by the Registrar-General in Malawi, Tanzania, Zambia and Zimbabwe; the Registrar of Births and Deaths in Botswana and Swaziland; the Director-General in South Africa; and the Registrar of Civil Status in Mauritius.[127] National death registers are compiled from returns of deaths supplied by district registrars. Swazi law also makes provisions for a separate register for "external deaths" in which deaths of citizens of Swaziland dying abroad are recorded.[128]

Duty to Register Deaths

In Mauritius, South Africa, Swaziland, Zambia and Zimbabwe, all deaths must be reported to the specified deaths registration officer.[129] In Malawi and Tanzania, the registration of deaths is compulsory if the deceased is of European, American and, in the case of Malawi, of Asiatic race or origin; or if the deceased is a native falling in the category of persons to whom the provisions relating to compulsory registration of births and deaths have been made applicable by the Minister.[130] Under Botswana's law, registration of deaths is voluntary except in districts in which such registration has been declared to be compulsory.[131]

Under the laws of Botswana, Malawi, South Africa, Tanzania, Zambia and Swaziland, the duty to give notice of death is given to relatives of a deceased person who were present at the death or in attendance during the last illness or at the dwelling with the deceased. In Tanzania and Malawi, this duty is restricted to "the nearest relatives" while in Botswana and Swaziland the duty applies to "every adult relative." Zambia imposes this duty on simply "every relative."

In default of such relatives, the duty to report the death rests with every person present at the death, or the occupier of the house in which such death occurred. In the inability or absence of such an occupier, the duty passes to any inmate of the dwellings, or any person finding or taking charge of the body, or causing the deceased to be buried. A similar provision is found under the Zimbabwe Act, which also adds headmen appointed under the Chiefs and Headmen Act of 1982 on the list of persons with duty to report deaths.[132] Under the law of Mauritius, a death must be reported by two persons who were present at the death or in attendance during the last illness; or by one person and the occupier of the house or premise where the death took place.[133]

Time Within Which Notice of Death Must be Given

Notice of death must be given within the prescribed time. In South Africa, death must be registered "as soon as is practicable" while, in Mauritius, this must be done within 24 hours. In Zimbabwe and Swaziland, the time within which deaths must be reported is five days and sixty days, respectively. The Swazi law extends this period to ninety days for deaths occurring abroad. In Botswana, Malawi, Tanzania and Zambia, the period set is one month. However, in Malawi and Tanzania this period can be extended to up to three months if the Registration Officer is satisfied that, for any cause, registration could not have been effected in one month.[134]

The laws set time periods after which registration of a death must follow a different procedure for "late registration." This usually involves obtaining the approval of the highest registration authority, i.e., the Registrar-General or Registrar, and proof of such material facts relating to such death to the satisfaction of the registration officer. In Botswana, Zambia and Zimbabwe, the above procedure must be followed if a death has not been reported within one year of its occurrence. In Malawi and Tanzania, this period is set at three months.[135]

Mode of Registration

Notice of death must also be given in the prescribed manner. Under the Malawi and Tanzanian legislation, a death may be registered in two different ways. The first is registration in person and the second is registration without personal attendance. Every person registering a death must, to the best of their knowledge and ability, give the prescribed particulars and must certify their correctness, either by signing or, if they are illiterate, by affixing their mark to the register. If the registration is affected without personal attendance, the person registering the death must sign or affix their mark to the prescribed form on which the prescribed particulars are reported to the District Registrar.[136] Under the proviso to Section 12 of the Malawi Act, delivery of a death report to a person for the time being employed in collecting revenue of the local authority for the area in which the death occurred, is deemed to constitute delivery of such report to the registration officer of the district in which such area is situated.

In Botswana, any person giving notice of a death who is not a medical practitioner must do so by either completing the prescribed form (Form B4) or verbally giving notice of the death to the District Registrar who then must complete the relevant form with respect to such death and cause it to be signed by the informant. When the person giving notice of death is a medical practitioner who dealt with the deceased before or after the death, he must complete a different form (B5), which, among other things, gives details of a medical nature.[137] A similar procedure is provided for under Sections 33 and 34 of the Zambian Act.

Under Section 16 of the Swazi Act, deaths occurring within Swaziland have to be reported to a registration officer or a chief of the area or his *induna* or a registration information officer nominated or appointed for this purpose. Within ten days of receiving such notice, the chief or his *induna* or a registration information officer must give written information of such death in the prescribed form to the registration officer of the district or sub-district in which the death occurred for registration.

As per Section 23 of the Act, an application to register a death of a Swazi citizen occurring abroad must be made in written form to the ambassador or such other representative of Swaziland as may be designated in the country where the person died. The death information form and the prescribed fee must accompany the application. An ambassador to whom such an application is made must forthwith transmit the application and the fee to the Registrar who in turn must enter the relevant information in the external death register.

Under the Zimbabwe Act, the giving of notice by any responsible person in the described manner is a sufficient discharge of the duty of that person as well as that of any other person to give notice of that particular death.[138] When the body of the deceased person has been examined by a medical practitioner, such medical practitioner must issue a death certificate which must be forwarded with the application to register the death of the person whose body was so examined.[139]

In South Africa, notice of death must be given by means of a certificate issued by a medical practitioner who either attended the deceased before his death or examined the corpse thereafter. The certificate must state the cause of death. This requirement is dispensed with only where no medical practitioner attended the deceased or examined his or her corpse.[140] Similarly, registration of a death occurring in Mauritius is done by producing a medical certificate of the cause of the death together with the deceased's birth/marriage certificate or National Identity Card. If a death occurs on board any ship or aircraft, the master of the ship must draw up a declaration of the death and, on arrival of the ship in Mauritius, must deliver the declaration to the Director of shipping who in turn must transmit the same to the Registrar of Civil Status for registration.[141]

Contents of an Entry

The information commonly required to be supplied for the purposes of registering a death includes: serial/entry number; name and surname of the deceased; age; sex; full address/residence; nationality; profession or occupation of the deceased; date, place and cause of death; and the signature, full name, address and profession or occupation of the informant and the signature of the registering officer.[142] In addition to the above, the Mauritius Act requires the entry in the Death Register to also mention the cause of death, the names of the spouse of the deceased if he or she had been married, the names of the parents of the deceased and the place of birth of the deceased.[143] Zambia too requires the cause of death as well as the social security details to be stated.

The Evidential Value of Death Certificates

After a death has been registered, a death certificate can be issued to the informant, or to any other person, in the latter case upon receiving a written application accompanied by the appropriate fee. The death certificate may be required to, among other things, obtain a burial permit.

Different legislation assigns different evidential value to death certificates. As with birth certificates, the legislation that assigns the strongest value to death certificates is the Mauritius Act whose Section 10(1) provides that "every certificate under the hand of the Registrar of Civil Status or an officer shall be evidence, until the contrary is proved...." This is followed by the laws of Botswana, Malawi, South Africa, Swaziland, Zambia and Zimbabwe under which a death certificate duly issued only constitutes *prima facie* evidence of the particulars set forth therein in all courts of law and public offices.[144] Other laws such as the Tanzania Ordinance are silent on the issue of the evidential value of death certificates. However, under the country's Evidence Act of 1967, the death register is, at the very least, admissible in evidence as a public record prepared in the normal course of business and whose entries must be presumed to be correct.

CONCLUSION

The foregoing survey of laws relating to registration and identification is relevant to immigration regimes. Registration of births and deaths is relevant to immigration because, as was seen in Chapters 1 and 2, there is a close relationship between immigration and citizenship. Citizenship in turn is closely tied to birth. Consequently, a sound system of registration of births and deaths can play an important part in establishing a sound immigration regime.

The system of registration of births and deaths also facilitates the system of general registration and identification, which is important to the immigration regime as all the information that is required for registration of births is also required for general registration, as is some of the information that goes in death registers. Indeed, many population registers are compiled on the basis of information contained in birth and death registers. In some countries, the requirement to place the entire contents of birth and death registers is found in the birth and death legislation itself. An example of this is the South African Act whose Section 5(3) provides that particulars obtained from documents relating to births and deaths furnished under the Act, as well as records of any births and deaths preserved in terms of the repealed Acts, "shall be included in the population register." It is such inclusion that actually constitutes the registration of those particulars. In some other countries such as Namibia and Swaziland, it is the general registration laws that require that the details supplied for registration must include, among other things, "the particulars required to be furnished when notice of birth is given."[145]

The information included in the population register from the birth and death registers is likely to be more accurate and reliable than that obtained from other means such as statements by adult persons which may be distorted to suit particular ends. That may explain the difference in the evidential value attached to population registers in various countries with different systems of compiling the information. In short, a good system of registration of births, marriages and deaths can greatly improve the efficiency and reliability of the general registration and identification system.

The legislation relating to registration and identification of persons in the SADC region presents a mixed picture. Most legislation relating to registration of births and deaths is fairly modern and covers the basics of a sound regime for such registration. Most has provisions which, if fully applied, can guarantee the accuracy and reliability of the contents of the registers. However, some other legislation leaves a lot to be desired. Some is too old, more attuned to the circumstances and concerns at the time it was first enacted almost a century ago than to modern issues. Some other laws, both modern and old, have provisions that give the impression that fathers have superior rights or are more authoritative with regard to matters pertaining to giving notice of births and deaths and changes of names of children born within wedlock. Such gender insensitive provisions may not pass the constitutional muster.

In some jurisdictions, registration of births and deaths is only compulsory in specified areas, which tend to be urban areas. However, in most jurisdictions visited, the immigration challenges were as acute in rural border areas as in urban areas. This is particularly so in countries that experience serious refugee problems.

The contents of birth and death registers do not carry equal evidential value in different SADC countries. In some, the contents of registers are sufficient evidence of what they contain. In others, such registers are only *prima facie* evidence of their contents. In other jurisdictions, no evidential value is attached to birth and death registers. This is not surprising given the differences in the quality of the systems of information collection, storage and retrieval.

There are considerable differences between the efficiency of the administrative arrangements put in place in various SADC countries to administer birth and death registers. Some countries have fairly sophisticated systems of information collection, storage and retrieval. In many others, the institutional arrangements for implementation of birth and death registration are weak and the resources devoted to it are inadequate.

Chapter 4 IMMIGRATION LAW AND POLICY

INTRODUCTION

The migration laws of the SADC countries have been changed more recently than their citizenship laws. At least five countries have significantly changed their migration laws within the past ten years: Mozambique, Namibia, South Africa, Tanzania, and Zimbabwe. Lesotho is presently in the midst of a fundamental revision of its laws. This phenomenon reflects both political factors (the post-apartheid governments in Namibia and South Africa) and economic factors (the more investor and business-friendly policies of Mozambique and Tanzania).

There are few multilateral international instruments that appear to be incorporated or used to any great extent in the migration regimes of the countries of SADC. This is in contrast to the refugee law regimes, where international instruments are depended upon heavily. South Africa's new Immigration Act 13 of 2002 is one of the few pieces of national immigration legislation in SADC that makes mention of any international instruments or the category of international instruments.[146] While Mozambique also explicitly refers to international agreements, the South African references are considerably more detailed.[147] One of the South African categories of temporary permits, treaty permits (Section 14), is entirely based on the existence of an international agreement to which South Africa is party. Furthermore, one part of the corporate permit (Section 21(4)) is apparently intended to continue the practice of employing migrant labourers in certain industries such as farming and mining.[148]

This does not mean that there are not international instruments that are relevant to national migration regimes. Apart from refugee-related international instruments and apart from regional instruments, there are two main categories of relevant multilateral international instruments.[149]

The first main set is those international instruments that regulate the treatment of migrant workers and their families.[150] The most important of these is the International Convention on the Protection of the Rights of All Migrant Workers and Members of Their Families (Adopted by General Assembly resolution 45/158 of 18 December, 1990). This convention is one of twelve international instruments followed closely by the United Nations Office of the High Commissioner for Human Rights (UNHCR) and is one of the twelve international human rights instruments that establish commissions to monitor compliance with the convention. Twenty countries have ratified the convention. Eleven other countries have signed the convention. The convention takes effect three months after twenty countries have ratified it and will come into operation soon. Only one country of the SADC region has ratified the convention: Seychelles on 15 December 1994. The principal International Labour Organisation (ILO) standards are the Migration for Employment Convention (Revised), 1949 (No. 97)[151] and the Migrant Workers (Supplementary Provisions) Convention, 1975 (No. 143).[152]

The second main set is those international instruments regulating international trade and services. In particular, the General Agreement on Trade in Services (GATS) provides a general framework for international agreements on trade-related temporary movements of people. At present, SADC has not yet established a free trade area in goods. However, SADC is discussing a free trade area in services, which would come into operation after the establishment of the free trade area in goods.[153]

There are additionally a number of bilateral international agreements that appear to play an important role in the functioning of migration regimes in the SADC region.[154] For instance, the bilateral labour agreements that South Africa has with Botswana, Lesotho, Swaziland, and Mozambique are important migration policy instruments. These agreements are discussed further below.

Other operational agreements may also exist at the bilateral level. Defence force or policing agreements may exist where security forces conduct or coordinate joint operations or border monitoring. For instance, in 2001, the Second Mozambique-South Africa Joint Commission was held. There are also trilateral agreements, such as the Agreed Minutes of the Trilateral Meeting among the Ministers of Home Affairs of Mozambique, Swaziland, and South Africa in Maputo on 1 April 1998.

Further, there are regular bilateral committee meetings at the operational level. The minutes of these meetings may constitute *de facto* and *de jure* international agreements regarding the operation of migration regimes. For instance, Mozambique participates in at least three such arrangements: the Sub-Committee on Migration and Labour between Mozambique and South Africa; the Sub-Committee on Defence, Security and Migration between the Kingdom of

Swaziland and the Republic of Mozambique; and the Sub-Committee on Migration, Security and Labour between Mozambique and Zimbabwe.[155] These sub-committees discuss issues such as the modalities and mechanisms for deportation, notification procedures to consulates, complaints against police and migration officials during the deportation process, legalisation of workers, and means for social integration of those repatriated. In another example, there are local operational agreements at the Ficksburg and the Maputsoe border posts between South Africa and Lesotho.[156]

SADC PROTOCOLS

This story of the origins and demise of the SADC[157] Draft Free Movement and Facilitation of Movement Protocols has been told elsewhere. At the present time discussion has been revived amongst member states through the SADC Organ. If the Facilitation Protocol were ever implemented, all countries would have a major challenge to bring their laws into harmony with each other and the Protocol.

However, this does not mean that there are no SADC regional instruments relevant to national migration regimes. A number of SADC Protocols contain provisions that are relevant to migration within the region. For instance, Article 3(a) of the SADC Protocol on Education and Training states as an agreed objective of Member States "to work towards the relaxation and eventual elimination of immigration formalities in order to facilitate freer movement of students and staff within the Region for the specific purposes of study, teaching, research and any other pursuits relating to education and training." In addition, the Protocol on Immunities and Privileges allows SADC to issue a SADC Laissez-Passer to its officials. Holders of the SADC Laissez-Passer have visa-free entry to the territory of all member states including persons holding a SADC Identity Card and travelling on the business of SADC.[158] Other relevant protocols such as one on social security are at a draft stage.

The relevance of these agreements is acknowledged and supported by some aspects of the national migration regimes. For instance, there are some references to the special position of the SADC in national migration policy frameworks. The Immigration Act (South Africa) recognizes the special position of SADC with respect to study, teaching, and research in the region.[159]

GROUNDS FOR EXCLUSION

In general, the migration policies of the SADC countries do not differ significantly in the grounds for exclusion that they adopt, at least within countries that come from the same legal tradition. As Table 9 shows, the countries of the British legal tradition have largely similar exclusion grounds. One of the categories of exclusion is on economic grounds. Nearly universally, the status of being likely to become a public charge leads to prohibited immigrant status. Additionally, a number of the laws allow for a person to be deemed prohibited on economic grounds such as having insufficient funds. In some of the legislation, the language of this ground for exclusion is exactly the same as the apartheid ground for exclusion: "deemed on economic grounds or standard or habits of life." When applied to a class of persons and when extending beyond economic grounds, the substantive policy of this ground for exclusion may be far-reaching. Given that women are more likely to be without economic resources than men, this ground for exclusion impacts on women more severely than men.

As a general matter, one can say that disease is grounds for exclusion from all SADC countries.[160] However, there is marked variety in the substance and the procedures for excluding persons on the grounds of disease. The formulation used in a number of statutes is that of infirmity of mind or body. Other laws include a provision excluding persons with a prescribed disease (e.g., Botswana). Some identify any infectious or contagious disease (e.g., Mauritius and Tanzania). Swaziland and Tanzania will exclude a person who refuses to submit to a medical examination after being required to do so. Some of the statutory grounds for exclusion that have been classified here as disease overlap with grounds of disability in terms of physical incapacity (e.g., Malawi). Many states use more than one of these disease-linked grounds for exclusion.

Likewise, a past criminal conviction will universally lead to prohibited immigrant status.[161] There is, however, variation in the kind of criminal conviction that qualifies. A number of countries rely on the fact of conviction without the option of a fine, while some others explicitly list crimes, a sentence for which leads to exclusion. While broadening the category of conviction to include the status where a warrant for arrest has been issued, South Africa explicitly includes international crimes such as genocide and torture on its list of crimes leading to exclusion. Zambia allows persons who are convicted criminals abroad to escape status as prohibited immigrants if they are of "good character." Mauritius, South Africa, and Tanzania specifically mention trafficking in drugs as grounds for exclusion, separate from the exclusion ground related to past criminal conviction.

National security is also a universal ground for exclusion. In a number of laws, however, the substantive ground is not explicitly included. Instead, it is likely to be included in the implicit grounds for a ministerial or presidential declaration deeming as undesirable. The parameters of this ground for exclusion are likely to be narrowed by courts through interpretation from the broad scope with which it is stated. For instance, the South African identification of membership in an association that uses crime or advocates racial hatred may be overly sweeping.

The prior violation of a migration law is a nearly universal ground for exclusion. To the extent that the criminal process has been used, this ground for exclusion may in some instances overlap with that of past criminal conviction or activity. While some of the statutes see any violation of migration laws as grounds for exclusion, others specify that only prior deportation (or being ordered to leave the country) or prior declaration as a prohibited immigrant would entail exclusion. Zambia invokes illegal entry, overstaying, and presence in Zambia for three months of 12 without a valid permit as grounds for exclusion. While they do not precisely fit into the category of prior violations of immigration laws, Swaziland treats failure to produce a passport and unlawful presence as worthy of exclusion.

With respect to prostitution and immorality, there is also a certain amount of variety. Four countries have no explicit ground for exclusion based on prostitution or living on the proceeds of prostitution: Lesotho, Namibia, South Africa, and Swaziland. Six others do. Further, Malawi and Zimbabwe specifically cite status as a homosexual as grounds for exclusion. The impact of the ground for exclusion of prostitution is likely to fall most heavily on women rather than on those men who also participate in trafficking and prostitution but without acting directly as sex workers.

Malawi is alone in determining illiteracy as a grounds for exclusion. Mauritius is the only country to identify habitual beggars, vagrants, and chronic alcoholics as persons liable to exclusion.

It should be emphasized that the above conclusion regarding the similarity of exclusion grounds is limited to those SADC countries within the British legal tradition. The exclusion grounds of Angola, the DRC and the Seychelles have not been determined. The immigration law of Mozambique does not have a set of exclusion grounds on the model of the British tradition, although article 16(1) is to much the same effect.

Finally, there is at least one significant variation with respect to the sphere of application of these grounds of exclusion.[162] Unlike other immigration laws, the Immigration Act 13 of 2002 (South Africa) essentially has two sets of exclusion grounds. The first are grounds that preclude a person from being granted a temporary or a permanent residence permit (Section 29). The second set of exclusion grounds put a person into a category of undesirable persons (Section 30). While status as a prohibited person is automatic, a person must be so declared by the Department in order to have the status as an undesirable person. There is a second difference between the two sets of exclusion grounds. Temporary residence permits are issued on the condition that persons are not and do not become either a prohibited or an undesirable person (Section 10(4)). Permanent residence permits may not be issued to prohibited persons (Section 25) although they may be issued to some categories of persons declared undesirable.

TEMPORARY RESIDENCE

We consider in this section all types of migration permits other than employment and investor permits as well as permits for permanent settlement.[163] Sometimes, persons who are granted a temporary residence permit for a purpose other than employment may also be granted permission to work. Certainly, many persons who are granted a temporary resident permit for a purpose other than employment do in fact work without authorization. Nonetheless, the distinction is worth making and we consider in the following two sections migration permits for employment/investor purposes and for permanent settlement.

As is clear from Table 10, there is a great variety in the permit classification used in the countries of SADC. That table was constructed using the categories of the Immigration Act (South Africa) as a guide. However, the table does not consider permits in three categories that are covered by the South African Act: diplomatic permits, crew permits, and transit permits. These categories are specialized ones that are covered in the temporary permit systems of the SADC countries in one way or another.

One important feature of the temporary residence permits is considered further in the section regarding migration permits for employment/investor purposes. This is whether or not the temporary residence permit is integrated with the employment/investor permit. Does a single document provide authorization for presence in the country's territory and at the same time authorize employment or investment activity? As discussed in the section on migration permits for employment/investor purposes, a number of the SADC countries have such an integrated temporary residence/work permit. That question of integration is discussed along with the operation of the visa system and its relationship to the system of temporary permits.

One important way in which the temporary permit systems of the SADC countries differ is with regard to their specificity. The South African temporary permit system is the most specific. It contains fifteen different types of permits. Other temporary permit systems are less specific. Part of the reason for this is that for most of the countries of the SADC region, the visitor's permit is a general-pur-

pose permit. This purpose may or may not be written on the visa/permit.[164] Used in this way, the general permit may serve the purpose of the more specific permits, although it does not serve to communicate the policy aims of the more specific categories. Once it is supplemented by regulations, the South African visitor's permit (discussed further below) plays both a specific and a general-purpose role.

All the SADC countries have some type of visitor's or general-purpose permit. In each case (except for Lesotho), there is a limit to the validity of this permit. The limits range from 90 days (Botswana, Malawi, Tanzania, and Zambia) to six months (DRC, Mauritius, Swaziland, and Zimbabwe) to 12 months (Namibia). In Mozambique, the visitor's permit is used for general purposes that do not fall within the business permit. The South African visitor's permit is really two types of permit. One is tenable for a maximum of 90 days; the other type, as supplemented by regulations and intended for various purposes, has a maximum of three years.

Many of the SADC countries have specific permits for study or educational purposes (DRC, Malawi, Mozambique, Namibia, South Africa, Swaziland, Zambia, and Zimbabwe). Zimbabwe has two types of study permit: one for scholars and one more general.

Tanzania is the only country besides South Africa to have what could be termed a treaty permit. For Tanzania, this is an Inter-State Pass, which allows for circulation among the countries of the East African region: Tanzania, Kenya, and Uganda. The South African category of permit is one that can be triggered by any present or future international agreement. It is not linked to any specific international agreement. Thus, the treaty permit may be used in South Africa to pursue SADC-related policy goals.

Zimbabwe is the only country besides South Africa to have a specific permit with respect to a person's health. The purpose behind the South African permit is to enable a person to receive medical treatment. The purpose of the Zimbabwean permit for a person with a prescribed disease appears to be to regulate the health risk posed by that person while still allowing them to enter Zimbabwe.

Many of the SADC countries have specific permits for the entrance of relatives. These provisions are likely to be used more by women than by men. Zambia makes a specific distinction between permits for the relatives of citizens and residents and the relatives of holders of temporary permits.

Finally, there are three categories of permits included in the new South African Immigration Act that do not have precise parallels in the specific temporary permits issued in any of the rest of the SADC countries. These purposes can of course be accommodated in the general-purpose visitor's permits. One of these categories is a retired person's permit, for an older person who intends to retire in the country. The second of these categories is an exchange permit. This is a permit that is linked to the operation of an international agreement of exchange, as for instance between two government departments of two different states. The existence of this separate category is likely to facilitate these kinds of department-to-department exchanges. The third and final category of permit is the cross-border pass. In the Immigration Act (South Africa), the cross-border pass is a form of identification that is issued by the South African authorities to residents of neighbouring countries and used for the purpose of crossing a specific border. Women from border regions may be particularly likely to use cross-border permits for the purpose of shopping, although there is evidence that women also participate in this regional trade in more long-term and long-distance enterprises. Again, it is likely that this kind of crossing-border purpose is accommodated within other permits that are available elsewhere in SADC.

There are two types of permits common in SADC countries that are not in use or no longer in use in South Africa. The first of these is the temporary permit issued to a prohibited person. This permit is available in Malawi, Swaziland, Tanzania, Zambia, and Zimbabwe. Moreover, it is likely more prevalent since it is essentially the same permit as the provisional pass that may be granted to a suspected prohibited immigrant during a process of examination at the border. This permit used to be granted in terms of Section 41 of the Aliens Control Act (South Africa). This Section 41 permit also fulfilled the function catered to by the special pass in two SADC countries (Swaziland and Tanzania). This special pass is designed to provide lawfulness to a person who is contesting a decision of the immigration authorities or who is awaiting a review of a decision by a higher authority within the immigration department (e.g., the Minister).

Finally, it should be noted that Tanzania has a category of re-entry permit which allows for a person to be easily identified as a person with a legal status that would permit that person to re-enter Tanzania after having departed.

EMPLOYMENT PERMITS, IMMIGRATION LAW AND VISAS

Table 11 indicates whether there are laws separate from the immigration laws that govern the employment or investment permits in the SADC countries; it also indicates the relationship between the visa system of a country (if any) and the system of temporary and employment permits. The existence of separate legislation for employment is significant in two ways. First, it indicates that there are separate permits required for residence and for employment or investment purposes. Second, the existence of separate legislation may indicate that there is a government department or ministry involved to some extent in the issuing of temporary residence permits.

There are at least five SADC countries that have separate legislation granting employment permits: Botswana, the DRC, Lesotho, Mauritius, and Mozambique. In Botswana, the Employment of Non-Citizens Act 11 of 1981 governs employment permits. In the DRC, separate laws govern general immigration and specific work permits. In Lesotho, the Department of Labour administers work permits in terms of its legislation. In Mauritius, the Non-Citizens Employment Restriction Act governs employment permits.[165] In Mozambique, Law 25/99 and 26/99 govern work visas. Nonetheless, the majority of the SADC countries' laws on immigration use an integrated system to grant permission for temporary employment, where the regulation of a person's right to enter and reside in the country is combined with the regulation of the right to work.

Even where there is no separate legislation, there may be involvement by a separate institution in decisions regarding employment permits. In Botswana, the Ministry of Home Affairs and Labour is a combined ministry. Nonetheless, a separate internal section of this Ministry deals with the administration of employment permits. In Swaziland, employment permits are decided upon with the help of the Ministry of Enterprise and Employment. Likewise, the Department of Labour is formally and specifically involved in several aspects of the issuance of work permits in terms of the Immigration Act (South Africa).[166]

Another significant aspect of the temporary permit system is the degree to which the system of visas is used. In many national migration regimes, visas are required (at least for citizens of certain countries) as a precondition in order to enter the country. In most SADC countries, the legal requirement of a "passport" for purposes of entry includes a visa in order to be a valid travel document (e.g., Section 12 of the Namibian legislation). However, the visa does not itself allow for admission into the country. For instance, a person with a visa may still be determined to be a prohibited immigrant on one or another grounds of exclusion.

While information is not available for Lesotho or Malawi, most countries use the visa system described above. In Botswana, Mauritius, Namibia, Swaziland, and Zambia, visas function as preconditions to the granting of temporary residence permits. However, in Tanzania, there is no visa system in the strict sense. Tanzanian temporary permits may be issued abroad or at the border. Similarly, in Mozambique, visas function as the temporary permit. There is also no visa system in Seychelles. In Zimbabwe, a passport may become a visitor's entry certificate upon endorsement at the border by an immigration official, even though a visa is apparently not required as a precondition.

South Africa, along with Zimbabwe, represents a combination of these models of visa systems. In South Africa, a visa is a required condition for the general-purpose visitor's permit for most persons. However, visas are not required for citizens of certain countries (as prescribed). Financial guarantees may be required for citizens of other countries (as prescribed). Until regulations are written and promulgated, it is not clear whether the South African system will require visas as a precondition for granting all the other types of temporary permits. However, it seems likely that South Africa will follow the Tanzanian/Mozambican/Zimbabwean model in part. Section 10(3) of the Act assumes that temporary residence permits may be issued abroad as well as within the South African territory.

Table 12 describes the substantive policies used in the granting of temporary employment permits in the SADC countries as well as the substantive policies on offer to attract investment and financial resources. In constructing this table, we have used five factors that are commonly used as part of a domestic labour market policy to regulate the employment of foreign workers: (i) the effect on domestic employment[167]; (ii) the condition of pre-entry engagement for employment; (iii) the limitation of a permit to a specific employer; (iv) the condition that the worker be paid a prevailing wage; and (v) the condition that the employer undertake specific training arrangements. In addition, some countries have the authority to limit the geographic area of the employment permit (e.g. Lesotho, Malawi).

Most countries explicitly take into account the effect of expatriate employment on domestic workers (Botswana, Lesotho, Malawi, Namibia, South Africa, Swaziland, and Zambia). This may be done either directly through the consideration of domestic employment as a factor in the decision to grant the work permit or indirectly through a requirement of diligent search for (South Africa) or advertisement for (Malawi) local workers. A number of countries specify that training arrangements for local workers are either positive factors or requirements (Botswana, Swaziland). Other countries may consider this factor in their general discretion. A requirement that a prevailing wage be paid is a factor only in South Africa. A few countries of the SADC region have a specific employer limitation as part of their employment permit (Malawi, Swaziland, Zimbabwe). Others require notification for a change in employment (South Africa).

To our knowledge, there are at least nine SADC countries with specific policies designed to attract investors or those persons with significant financial resources: Botswana, DRC, Malawi, Mauritius, South Africa, Swaziland, Tanzania, Zambia, and Zimbabwe.[168] In most of these countries, the permits are simply available upon payment of a particular fee (Malawi, Mauritius, South Africa, Swaziland, Tanzania, and Zambia). Zambia adds a requirement that the person's presence be a benefit to the inhabitants of the country generally. Although the use of the factor of wealth in immigration policy is formally gender-neutral, it should be recognized that there is a gendered effect. As Dodson points out, "the application of skill and wealth-based admission criteria would in effect serve to discriminate in favour of men."

BILATERAL LABOUR AGREEMENTS

There are a number of bilateral agreements that South Africa has used to regulate labour migration from neighbouring countries. The Mozambican agreement dates back to the early part of the century. Those with Botswana, Lesotho, and Swaziland regulate the border controls that were put in place in the 1960s. The Malawi agreement was in heavy use and is now apparently defunct.[169]

One of the uncommon features about the bilateral agreements presently operative between South Africa and Botswana, Lesotho, and Swaziland (although not that with Mozambique) is that repatriation regulation is dealt with in an agreement together with labour migration. For instance, the Government Labour Offices and Representatives established under these three agreements have the function to "assist the Government of the Republic of South Africa with the repatriation of sick, injured or destitute Swaziland citizens who are or were employed in the Republic of South Africa *and of other such citizens whose presence in the Republic of South Africa is or has become unlawful* (emphasis added)." Article 5 requires consultation with the Swaziland Representative before a Swazi citizen may be repatriated. While the focus of the agreements is on labour migration, others may be caught within its provisions.

There may be an immediate consequence of the placement of repatriation and labour policy within the same bilateral agreement. At least from the South African side, it will not be possible to simply roll over the existing bilateral agreements as the agreements contemplated in Section 21(4) of the Immigration Act.[170]

PERMANENT RESIDENCE[171]

As Table 13 shows, there is a fair amount of variation in the permanent residence policies of the SADC region. One country, Swaziland, does not even have this category of immigration status at all. Where the category exists, it is possible to distinguish two models. First, there is a model that treats permanent residence as an extension of temporary status. In a number of countries, the category of permanent resident is barely distinguished, if at all, from that of temporary resident: DRC, Mauritius, Tanzania, and Zambia. In two countries (Botswana and Namibia), the decisions about permanent resident permits are made by an independent and specialized entity: the Immigrants Selection Board.[172] However, in Namibia, the Immigrants Selection Board also makes decisions on temporary employment, straddling the line between temporary and permanent residence. In the second model, there is a sharp distinction between temporary and permanent residence. South Africa and Botswana have this model, where permanent residents are treated nearly as well as citizens. Lesotho also makes such a sharp distinction.

In both of these models, the acquisition of permanent residence status can either be an automatic or a discretionary decision. If it is automatic, the acquisition of permanent residence is usually dependent either on a number of years of lawful status or on family status. In the automatic granting of permanent residence based on years of lawful status, the number of years varies. In Botswana and Mozambique, 10 years of lawful status yields permanent residence. In South Africa, the figure is five (of work permit status) with an offer of permanent employment. Zimbabwe also has a five-year period for conversion, as a general rule. Family reunification is an explicit policy in South Africa and Zimbabwe. An explicit family reunification policy is likely to be favourable to women and to reconcile legal with social realities. The discretionary decision is the model present in Lesotho, South Africa (alongside the automatic model), Malawi, Namibia, Tanzania, and Zambia.

EXCLUSION PROCEDURES

As Table 14 shows, there is significant variety within the SADC countries regarding the procedures providing for exclusion and for expulsion. This table is constructed to show the potential linkage between the procedures and the grounds for exclusion and expulsion.[173] By "exclusion" we mean state action to deny a migrant entrance or admission into the country of migration. Terms that are used for exclusion are "deny admission" or "refusal to grant leave to enter." By "expulsion" we mean state action to deny a migrant continued presence within the country of migration. Terms that are used for expulsion are "required to leave," "ordered to leave," "removal," and "deportation."

When considering exclusion procedures, we can use the applicable international law standards as one form of measurement or comparison. It should be noted that international law hardly regulates the admission of persons at the border, even with respect to procedural requirements. However, it is typical for states to provide some sort of procedural protection for actions of exclusion, and the SADC countries are no exception to this international trend. Each country provides for some sort of exclusion procedure by law. The partial exceptions are Lesotho, where the exclusion procedures appear to be relatively informal and Mauritius, where the exclusion procedures consist largely of claiming residence or citizenship via an appeal to the Minister.

For almost all the SADC countries, there is a basic minimum requirement of written notification of the action of exclusion to the person who is excluded.[174] However, there is significant variation in the content of this written notification. In some countries, this written notification may be a bare notification of status (e.g., Swaziland). In some countries, the written notification of exclusion will at least need to identify the provision of law depended upon in order to exclude a person from entry (e.g., Malawi, Zimbabwe). In some other countries (Botswana), the written notification must include the grounds for exclusion. The Botswana Notice of Determination as Prohibited Immigrant uses the term "reasons" as well as mentioning the provisions of the Act and contains four lines where the Immigration Officer may fill in the grounds/reasons for the determination. Under this formulation, it is possible that a requirement to give reasons for the exclusion decision is a matter of law in Botswana.[175] The South African position under the new legislation is still unclear. The Immigration Act provides for notification in writing of rights and "other prescribed matters" upon exclusion.[176]

A second element of the usual exclusion procedures in the SADC countries is the opportunity to receive a provisional permit. The purpose of this provisional permit is to allow the Immigration Officer to conduct an investigation in order to determine whether the applicant is or is not to be excluded. It also functions in Zambia as a means to allow an applicant to submit written representations to the minister after seven days of lawful presence in the country.

The provisional permit is a common but clearly not universal procedure. This element exists in Mauritius, Namibia, Swaziland, Zambia, and Zimbabwe. There is no such procedure in Botswana, South Africa or Tanzania.[177] The time limits on such a provisional pass vary from 30 days (Zambia) to three months (Swaziland). Additionally, Zimbabwe limits the availability of such a provisional pass to persons who have action taken against them in terms of certain grounds of exclusion.

A third element of the national exclusion procedures commonly used is the opportunity for representations to the Minister. The time limit on these opportunities for representations is generally three days. Zimbabwe gives a right of representation of 24 hours with respect to most of the grounds for exclusion, but there is no right to representation for persons excluded on economic grounds or that of a past criminal conviction or by ministerial deeming order. In some countries, the opportunity to make representations is given with respect to some commonly used grounds for exclusion as an apparent alternative to the usual procedures of appeal to a magistrate's court (Malawi).

In South Africa, the opportunity to make representations to the Minister is preceded by the opportunity (but also the requirement) to make representations to the Director-General. This is part of the package of adjudication and review procedures applicable generally to all immigration decisions. If, after ten days, there is no response to the appeal/representation to the Director-General, the decision to exclude is taken as confirmed. The applicant then has the opportunity to appeal to the Minister, who after 20 days without response can also be taken to have confirmed the decision. In this procedure, there is explicitly no obligation on the Director-General or the Minister to respond to the appeals.

A fourth element of exclusion procedures is the possibility of an appearance in, or an appeal to, the court structures. The immigration laws of some countries explicitly preclude appeal to a court. There is a blanket preclusion in Swaziland. Namibia does not allow an appeal to the courts with respect to exclusion, depending instead on its procedure of issuing a two-month provisional permit during an investigation as well as on its expulsion procedure where review by an immigration tribunal is central. In a similar policy, South Africa only allows an appeal to the magistrate's court after exhaustion of remedies in front of the Director-General and the Minister.

In several countries, an appeal to a court is allowable with respect to exclusion decisions (at least on some grounds) but must be noted within three days of exclusion (Botswana, Malawi, Zimbabwe). Tanzania allows persons who have been refused entry to demand to be taken in front of a magistrate (unless they are persons who have been declared to be prohibited).

EXPULSION PROCEDURES

When considering the expulsion procedures on their own, we can use the international law standards for expulsion as one form of measurement.[178] One source for the international law standards is Article 13 of the International Covenant on Civil and Political Rights. In terms of this Article, at least for persons who are legally within the territory of the country, expulsions must be governed by procedures that are established by law with some opportunity for the person expelled

to submit reasons against the expulsion and some kind of review by and representation before a competent authority. Even these requirements (except for that of establishment by law) can be relaxed in cases of national security. As with exclusion procedures, most of the international community and the SADC countries have established national procedures that go beyond these minimum international requirements.

Most expulsions in the SADC region appear to be what one might term voluntary repatriations. When, for instance, a Lesotho citizen who has overstayed a permit in South Africa presents himself or herself at the border, the immigration authorities will most likely simply allow that person to return to Lesotho.[179] While there is no specific evidence to back up this point, it is likely that this sort of voluntary repatriation is more likely to include disproportionate numbers of female as opposed to male migrants. This section does not describe the procedures in practice for this sort of "voluntary repatriation" and instead details the more formal deportation procedures.

All the SADC countries probably meet the international requirement of a procedure established by law for expulsion, though shortfalls exist in many countries with respect to the public availability of laws, regulations, and procedures. The international requirement for an opportunity to submit reasons against expulsion and for review by and representation in front of a competent authority can also be met either by the model of appeal to a magistrate's court (used at least as a general matter in Botswana, Malawi, Namibia,[180] and Zimbabwe[181]) as well as by the model of representations to the Minister (used in Mauritius and Swaziland, in certain cases). In Mauritius and Swaziland, the Minister benefits from a magisterial or administrative report or recommendation. Tanzania, Swaziland, and Zambia come closest to the international minimum standards, apparently requiring only notification or warrants for some of those persons subject to expulsion. Mozambique and South Africa combine the two models of internal administrative review and external judicial review. Mozambique allows for either an internal appeal or a judicial one or possibly both. South Africa allows clearly for a judicial appeal but only after at least 30 days of consideration by the administrative and Ministerial authorities.

THE LINKAGE BETWEEN EXCLUSION AND EXPULSION

The relationship between exclusion grounds and procedures and the grounds and procedures for expulsion is close in a number of SADC countries. For some countries, this relationship is close because of the grounds for state action (Botswana, Malawi, Namibia, South Africa, and Zimbabwe). In other countries (and some of the same countries), this relationship is close because of the procedures for exclusion and expulsion (Botswana, Lesotho, Malawi, South Africa, and Zimbabwe). Indeed, in at least two SADC countries (Botswana and Malawi), the immigration laws seem to treat both the grounds and the procedures for exclusion and expulsion as alike. In only one SADC country (Mauritius) are there different laws for exclusion and expulsion.

The linkage between exclusion and expulsion grounds is often a matter of the status of prohibited immigrants. What matters is status as a prohibited immigrant. A prohibited immigrant will be both excluded and expelled. This underlying status of prohibited immigrant is at work in several countries: Botswana, Malawi, Namibia, South Africa, and Zimbabwe. Even where status as a prohibited immigrant is not nearly completely identified with the grounds for expulsion, it does largely overlap with those grounds as in Mauritius, Swaziland, Tanzania, and Zambia. Lesotho does not work with the concept of the "prohibited immigrant," working instead with the even more basic notion of unlawfulness. Mozambique works in the opposite direction from the prohibited immigrant concept; there, grounds for expulsion serve as potential grounds for exclusion as well.

The expulsion procedures are the same as the exclusion procedures in two countries simply due to this concept of prohibited immigrant status (Botswana and Malawi). In other countries, there are relatively minor differences between these two procedures (Zambia and Zimbabwe).[182]

By comparison with exclusion procedures, expulsion procedures differ significantly only where there is another body or institution brought into play. In Mauritius, a magistrate is involved in expulsion but not in exclusion. In Tanzania, the opposite holds true; a magistrate is at least potentially involved in exclusion but not in expulsion. In Namibia, the Immigration Tribunal is involved in expulsion but not in exclusion. Likewise in Swaziland, albeit at a more informal level, the Immigration Advisory Committee is involved only in expulsions.

DETENTION[183]

As Table 15 shows, only two SADC countries have the same statutory rules to govern detention at the border and detention pending expulsion: Lesotho and South Africa. In both cases, the procedures used are likely to differ at the level of regulations and operating procedures. This is hardly surprising given the different administrative problems posed by the two different situations.[184]

Most SADC countries specify a relatively short period of time for detention of persons at the border. The general limit is 14 days (Botswana, Malawi, Namibia, Zambia, and Zimbabwe). A number of countries will allow for an extension of the period of detention by ministerial order (Botswana and Namibia). Tanzania has no explicit limit, but the custody is implicit in the process of being conducted across the frontier and may be assumed to be relatively short (unless the person is declared a prohibited immigrant and taken into formal custody). There are some exceptions to the relatively short detention for exclusion. The South African limit for detention at the border is 30 days without a court warrant, although there is a procedure whereby a detainee may request an earlier warrant to confirm his or her detention. Swaziland says that custody may be "as long as necessary." The limit of Mauritius depends on the decision of the Minister.

The place of detention at the border is very broad. In some formulations it may be either a prison or a gaol (Botswana, Malawi). In Swaziland, the custody for persons detained at the border is police custody. Other countries note that the place of detention may be some other prescribed place (Lesotho) or do not specify the place of detention (Mauritius, Namibia, and Tanzania). Zambia allows for detention at a public place with detention facilities and Zimbabwe allows for detention at some other convenient place. South Africa provides the only explicit mention of a minimum standard of detention, mandating minimum prescribed standards of detention protecting the dignity and "relevant" human rights of the detainee. At the level of statute, there is no explicit mention of different facilities or detention conditions for women and men.

In many countries of the SADC region, a statutory provision allows for a bond to be paid in place of detention for persons who are arrested at the border (Botswana, Malawi, Namibia, and Zimbabwe). In South Africa, a person can be forced to pay costs of detention, without necessarily securing his or her release from detention.

In general, the period of time allowed for detention pending expulsion is not specified. This is presumably a realistic response to the administrative difficulties of arranging for repatriation of detainees. In some countries, the period of time is not stated (Lesotho, Malawi, and Namibia). In a number of countries where the period of time is addressed by statute, the formulation used reflects the administrative nature of the detention. In Botswana, the period is any period as necessary; in Swaziland the period is "until his departure." In Zambia and Zimbabwe, the administrative nature of this standard is expressed in the legislation: the period of time for detention pending expulsion is pending the completion of arrangements for the removal or deportation. In some countries (Mauritius and Tanzania), the time periods vary as to whether the expulsion is ordered through the court system or through the administrative department.

In some countries, the range of places where detainees may be held pending expulsion is narrower than where they may be held when arrested at the border (Botswana and Malawi). In others, the same terms are used (South Africa, Zambia, Zimbabwe).

In Mauritius, Namibia, and South Africa, the court system has a built-in role in monitoring the length of detention pending expulsion.

REGULATION OF DEPARTURE

As Table 16 shows, there is generally relatively light regulation of departures from SADC countries of both their citizens and non-citizens.[185] In general, the kind of action that is required is merely the production of a valid passport or travel document, filling in a report of departure, and effecting the departure through a mandated port of entry.[186] In a couple of countries, the departure of persons appears to be largely unregulated (Lesotho and Tanzania). In Zimbabwe, however, the departure of persons is highly regulated with five separate sections of the migration legislation devoted to the process of examining and permitting departures.[187] Like many other SADC countries, Zimbabwe follows the norm in regulating departure within the ambit of its principal immigration legislation. However, Malawi, Mauritius, Namibia and Swaziland use legislation additional to the principal immigration legislation to regulate departure.

The principal exception to the norm is Malawi where the African Emigration and Immigration Workers Act 1 of 1954 aims, in part, to control the emigration of workers (essentially to South Africa).[188] The Act requires adult males to have identity certificates authorizing them to leave Malawi (s 4); women may accompany or have their own certificate. To the extent that the Act is implemented with women having a migration status dependent upon that of specific men, it presents the opportunity for restricting the freedom of movement of women. This Act worked with and facilitated the operation of the bilateral labour agreement between Malawi and South Africa.

OFFENCES, PENALTIES AND SANCTIONS

There is not a great variety in the offences identified and punished in the migration laws of SADC. Table 17 describes the criminal offences and penalties applicable in the region. General migration offences such as falsification of documents

and providing false information to an immigration officer are universally proscribed. Maximum terms of imprisonment for this sort of migration crime range from up to 12 months (Malawi, Swaziland, Zambia) to up to five years (Lesotho). Bribing or influencing an immigration officer is also commonly criminalized.

Criminal sanctions in the migration laws are sometimes used to deal with the situation of illegal employment. In South Africa, Swaziland, and Zambia, it is an offence to employ persons unlawfully present.

There are numerous countries that criminalize aiding and abetting unlawful entry. However, there are no countries in the SADC region that criminalize trafficking on its own. This question is discussed further below in the section on anti-trafficking.

The greatest variation in the types of offences is in the South African law. The South African law goes considerably further than any other law in the SADC region and attempts to use the criminal law to govern the provision of state services. Thus, the intentional facilitation of receipt of public services by an "illegal foreigner" is criminal in terms of Section 49(4).

Within the category of violations of migration statutes, one can make a distinction between administrative offences and criminal offences.[189] This is a distinction that is made explicitly only in Mozambique (where some offences are referenced to the Criminal Code) and in South Africa (where a few offences are specifically identified as administrative offences). Criminal offences are usually punished with fines and/or sentences of imprisonment. Administrative offences are punished with fines only. The value of making the distinction between criminal and administrative offences is that it is easier for immigration authorities to impose the administrative offences because the criminal procedure protections and judicial process do not have to be directly used.

TRAFFICKING

The issue of human trafficking has recently risen to prominence on the international legal agenda. For instance, two 2001 international instruments concern the problem of human trafficking.[190] In addition, the United States Department of State has embarked upon a major effort to strengthen laws against trafficking in persons, reporting in 2001 and 2002 on a country by country basis on the effectiveness of national laws to combat trafficking. The UNHCR has recently reported on a set of principles and guidelines recommended to prevent trafficking and safeguard the human rights and dignity of those trafficked.

The accepted international law definition of human trafficking refers to "the recruitment, transportation, transfer, harbouring or receipt of persons, by means of the threat or use of force or other forms of coercion, of abduction, of fraud, of deception, of the abuse of power or of a position of vulnerability or of the giving or receiving of payments or benefits to achieve the consent of a person having control over another person, for the purpose of exploitation."[191] As the UNHCR report goes on to explain: "Trafficking means much more than the organized movement of persons for profit. The critical additional factor that distinguishes trafficking from migrant smuggling is the presence of force, coercion and/or deception throughout or at some stage in the process—such deception, force or coercion being used for the purpose of exploitation."

Using this definition, the component offences of trafficking include the recruitment, transportation, transfer, harbouring or receipt of persons (over the age of eighteen years or children) by means of threat, force, coercion or deception for the purpose of exploitation.

As mentioned above, there is no specific criminalization of trafficking in the national legislation of the SADC region. However, there are criminal offences provided for that come close to elements of the crime of trafficking. The closest typical offence is that of aiding and abetting the unlawful entry of persons. However, there are some statutes that get more specific than this. Mauritius potentially addresses the element of providing benefits to those with control over persons and criminalizes assisting of entry or departure for money. In addressing the specific element of transportation, Namibia criminalizes conveying unlawful entrants (s 56(b)), classifying that crime within the same range as its other migration crimes. A couple of countries criminalize harbouring: Swaziland and Tanzania.

It may be useful to know to what extent trafficking is perceived to be a problem in the SADC region. Three countries in the SADC region are covered in the 2002 US *Trafficking in Persons (TIP) Report:* Angola, South Africa, and Tanzania. According to the 2002 TIP Report, each of these countries is a Tier 2 country. This means that in the published view of the US Department of State, "the country does not yet fully comply with the minimum standards for the elimination of trafficking; however it is making significant efforts to do so."[192]

According to the 2002 TIP Report, "Angola is a country of origin for persons trafficked primarily to South Africa and Mozambique. Much of Angola's trafficking problem has been related to its civil war, which ended with an April 2002 cease-fire. During the civil war children were abducted by the UNITA rebel movement for use in forced labor and in military service. UNITA trafficked women for forced labor and sexual exploitation."

The Report also notes that: "South Africa is a destination country for women, mainly between 18 and 25 years old, from other parts of Africa, Eastern Europe, Asia, and the former Soviet Union. South African women also are trafficked internally. Trafficking syndicates bring most of the women to Johannesburg, Cape Town, Durban, Pretoria and Port Elizabeth for work in the sex industry. South Africa is also a transit point for trafficking operations between developing countries and Europe, the United States and Canada."

The Report states: "Tanzania is a source country for trafficked persons. Available information indicates that trafficking in Tanzania is most often internal and related to child labor, including child prostitution in the larger cities. Some sources also suggest that women and girls may be trafficked to South Africa, the Middle East, North Africa, Asia, and Europe to work as prostitutes. Children are trafficked from rural to urban areas within the country for domestic work, commercial agriculture, fishing, and mining. Children in the country's large refugee population are especially vulnerable to being trafficked to work on Tanzanian plantations, and some have been transported from refugee camps for training as child soldiers. To a lesser degree, Tanzania is a destination point for trafficked persons from India and surrounding African countries."

Our surveys focused on the issue of trafficking in women and children. In general, trafficking was not perceived to be a pressing problem in our country interviews.[193] Trafficking is not perceived as a problem in Botswana, Lesotho, and Swaziland. Trafficking was a matter of concern in Namibia, where the difficulty in distinguishing between trafficking and economic migrancy was noted.[194] In Mozambique, the trafficking of women from Mozambique to Johannesburg was noted.

In conclusion, we would note that trafficking is an area of policy where the dual vulnerabilities of gender and migration are most apparent. Trafficking (and the lack of anti-trafficking provisions in SADC) impacts on women and vulnerable populations in two specific ways. (With respect to persons in vulnerable situations, these impacts may also be felt by men.) First, women and children are most likely to be trafficked. They are both the stuff and the victims of trafficking. Steps to address trafficking mostly stop trafficking in women and children.

Second, however, there are gender issues in the ways to address trafficking. We have noted that the standard international set of remedies for the problem of trafficking may be critiqued from a gender point of view. What is generally not taken into account are the rights of the victims; of the trafficked themselves. Most often these victims are women. One example of their rights not being taken into account is the speed with which women who are trafficked are deported back to their countries of origin. Also, there are rights of dignity for the victims of trafficking that can and should be respected as the SADC region comes to terms with the migration issue of trafficking.

XENOPHOBIA

Xenophobia is a phenomenon that is often recognized as a social ill in the same vein as racism and gender discrimination. There is specific policy reference to the need to combat xenophobia in the Immigration Act (South Africa). Clause (m) of the Preamble states that the new system of immigration control should ensure that "xenophobia is prevented and countered both within Government and civil society." However, the South African Human Rights Commission has taken the position that other provisions and mechanisms in the Act (particularly the community enforcement approach) are most likely to increase and not decrease xenophobia.

While not reporting xenophobia in their own countries, officials from some neighbouring countries noted their perceptions of the prevalence of xenophobia in South Africa. In Lesotho, the problem of xenophobia, while not serious, was acknowledged to be subtle and present. Asian persons were mentioned as targets of xenophobia. In Mozambique, the phenomenon of labour xenophobia was acknowledged. A recent SAMP survey of xenophobic attitudes in seven SADC countries shows that there is no room for complacency. Intolerance of outsiders is indeed strong and pervasive in South Africa. Namibian citizens' attitudes are also rather intolerant, with the situation in Botswana declining rapidly. In other countries surveyed (Mozambique, Swaziland and Zimbabwe), attitudes are much more relaxed. The authors of that report suggest that all countries need to take the problem seriously since it runs counter to the spirit and reality of regional cooperation and integration.[195]

GENDER AND MIGRATION

Our study confirms that research into formal labour migration leads to a relative neglect of women in regional migration studies. Most officials emphasized simply that there is no formal discrimination: "just the same, no special treatment." Similarly, the trend in the region has been towards the use of gender neutral language in legislation.[196] Throughout this report, however, we have attempted to note explicitly a number of instances where either formal equality or the lack of a formal policy at all may be an indication of a differential (and negative) impact

on women.[197] Undoubtedly, there are more instances than we have specifically noted.

The negative impacts of migration practices on women's lives can be identified when one realizes that gender and migration are often dual and intersecting vulnerabilities.[198] For instance, the lack of cross-border permits undoubtedly makes the significant number of cross-border traders (largely, though not exclusively, women) subject to corruption and legalistic obstacles in their attempts to engage in informal sector, unskilled economic activity. In much formal research and policy, gender is thus a factor of commission and omission.[199]

One clear issue directly concerning gender did emerge from the country interviews: the matter of marriages of convenience.[200] Most of the countries under study felt that changes in the law were necessary to deal with this matter, although there was no consensus on the direction to be taken. One aspect of this is the acquisition of citizenship by marriage. Namibia is amending its law to provide for acquisition of citizenship only after seven years instead of the present two years. It is felt that this will protect Botswana women from foreign men. Some women have asked for help from the Department of Home Affairs in enforcing agreements of marriage for payment. Since acquisition of citizenship by marriage is gender-neutral, this amendment is apparently gender-neutral, also affecting foreign women who marry Namibian men.

Another aspect of the matter of marriages of convenience is the renunciation of citizenship that can be linked to marriage. Lesotho, for example, requires that its citizens who marry other citizens and acquire dual citizenship renounce one or the other. However, since 1989, women are allowed two years (rather than three months) to effect this renunciation, in order to make certain that the marriage is a good one.

IMPLEMENTING INSTITUTIONS

It is a universal feature of migration legislation implementation that the police are involved. For the most part, it would appear that general police policies regarding arrest, detention and related matters apply to police action taken in terms of the migration regime.[201] Although used in more limited instances, national defence forces also frequently implement immigration laws. To a lesser extent, this feature holds for the prison service as well. This report has, however, not investigated the policies under which foreign criminals are held and deported.

As discussed more fully above in the section on employment permits, the function of labour migration often leads to implementation by agencies other than immigration departments in the receiving country.

Labour migration may also lead to institutional differentiation in the sending country. In particular, Angola and Mozambique appear to differ significantly from other SADC countries. They both have a government body that is competent to deal with the affairs of their citizens abroad. For instance, the main function of INAME of Mozambique is to look after the well-being of Mozambican nationals in South Africa and elsewhere. However, at least some SADC countries have bodies that perform at least part of these functions. The bilateral agreements discussed above establish Government Labour Offices and Representatives for Botswana, Lesotho, and Swaziland.

Exemplifying a trend within the public service, a function of the Immigration Act (South Africa) is to privatize the implementation of immigration control. Section 2(2)(k) allows the Department of Home Affairs to "be empowered to contract through public tender with private persons to perform under its control any of its functions, including but not limited to detaining and escorting illegal foreigners for deportation purposes and manning ports of entry." Other sections of the Act mandate private institutions to perform the administrative work of migration management, such as allowing institutions of learning to perform much administration with respect to study permits.

BUDGETING AND COST RECOVERY

The use of legislative provisions for cost recovery is undoubtedly pursued the most aggressively in the recent South African legislation. Section 2(1)(k) gives one of the objectives and functions of the Department of Home Affairs to be "administering the prescribed fees, fines and other payments [the Department] exacts or receives in such a fashion as to defray the overall cost of its operation." True to this spirit, a number of provisions specifically are designed to recover costs. For instance, Section 34(3) allows the Department to order a foreigner subject to deportation to deposit funds sufficient to cover the foreigner's costs of deportation. Likewise, certain citizens from certain countries may be required to post financial guarantees in order to gain admission on a visitor's permit (Section 11(1)(b)).

A distinction should be made between cost recovery of deportation costs and carrier sanctions. Carrier sanctions go further than cost recovery. Carrier sanctions cost more money than the money used to transport the person denied admission back to the country of origin. In general, the countries of the SADC are legally empowered to recover the costs of repatriation from carriers. However, only South Africa has the statutory authority to levy a modest sanction (R8000) on the carrier.

CONCLUSION

By way of conclusion to this chapter, we attempt to classify the SADC national migration regimes into three types: control-oriented, regulative, and facilitative. There are many ways to do such a classification and our classification is only one of many possible classifications. In making up our classification, we have not considered a country's policy with respect to refugees. Nor have we considered a country's nationality or immigrant integration policies. Instead, we have looked at a country's policy in the areas covered by this report: permanent and tempo-rary migration policy (including employment migration) and rights-regarding enforcement of the problem of undocumented migration.

One matter that we have not canvassed is policy towards levels of immigration and emigration. In 1996, Namibia reported to the United Nations Population Division that it sought to raise the level of migration for permanent settlement. It was the sole country in the SADC country to report that policy and one of only two countries in Africa to report that policy.[202] It is unclear (but it seems unlike-ly) whether this remains the migration policy of Namibia. In any case, our classi-fication depends not upon such a general policy but rather on a specific intra-regional comparison (e.g., among the SADC countries).

Our classification is also not the more usual one between labour-exporting and labour-importing countries. Within the SADC region, this has usually meant a divide between South Africa as a labour-importing country and all other SADC countries as labour-exporting countries, although some other SADC countries are recognized as being situated on the receiving end of migrant streams: the DRC, Tanzania, Zambia and Zimbabwe.[203]

With respect to temporary and permanent migration policy, an important fea-ture is the integration of employment and immigration status. Botswana, the DRC, Lesotho, Mauritius, and Mozambique do not have such integration. Swaziland does not have such integration in practice. With respect to rights-regarding enforcement, only Namibia and South Africa have explicit legal safe-guards of human rights of migrants.

In this rough and ready classification, either steps towards a rights-regarding migration enforcement or use of an integrated permit system or both factors will gain a country mention as regulative rather than control-oriented. But to be facilitative requires demonstrated cooperation with neighbouring or regional partner countries. We end up by placing no countries in the facilitative category. We place Namibia, the Seychelles and South Africa in the regulative category. We place Botswana, the DRC, Lesotho, Malawi, Mozambique, Swaziland, Tanzania, Zambia, and Zimbabwe as control-oriented.

Chapter 5

REFUGEES AND IMMIGRATION CONTROLS

INTRODUCTION

In a non-technical sense, a "refugee" refers to a person who has fled to a country that is not his or her own for the purposes of seeking asylum. Refugee movements are relevant to the immigration regime for a number of reasons. First, a refugee movement is by definition an international migratory movement. To be a refugee, a person must be outside their country of nationality or habitual residence. In other words, to be a refugee, a person must move across an international frontier.

Second, as we point out in the chapter on citizenship, international law vests the exclusive right and duty to protect persons in the state of which they are nationals. This includes when nationals are outside their own countries. However, this norm is fundamentally affected by refugee status in that, to be refugees, people must have lost the protection of their own country. Refugee law stipulates norms under which refugees get surrogate protection from the international community.

Third, refugee treaties and domestic legislation provide for different procedures for admission of asylum seekers that are less restrictive than those which apply to people generally under immigration laws. The nature and quality of these procedures can have an impact on current migration problems. For example, lax asylum procedures can be abused by economic migrants to enter other states and enjoy the benefits from which they would otherwise be excluded by immigration law. Conversely, overly restrictive immigration procedures can lead asylum seekers to turn to human traffickers to reach countries of asylum. Once in the country of asylum, trafficked persons may decline to declare their presence for fear of being penalized for illegal entry.[204] This ultimately undermines immigration management, the objective of which is to ensure that every foreign person in the country is documented.

Also, refugee law enjoins states to guarantee refugees certain minimum conditions of sojourn including with regard to freedom of movement and engagement in gainful employment. Differential treatment of refugees in various countries is known to be a cause of irregular movement of asylum seekers and refugees.

For the above reasons, the quality of refugee legislation has an impact on the efficiency of immigration regimes.

The overwhelming majority of SADC countries have ratified the key international instruments relating to refugees and have enacted legislation to deal with the phenomenon. Of the eleven pieces of legislation studied, two were enacted in the 1970s, three in the 1980s and six in the 1990s. All the legislation, with the exception of that enacted in the 1970s, has provisions that largely reflect standards found under international refugee instruments. Even in countries where the legislation does not reflect international standards, the practice on the ground is that the principles of international protection are adhered to.

Unlike typical work on refugee law, the purpose of this section is not to examine whether and to what extent the arrangements for the protection of refugees in SADC countries are adequate. Rather, the purpose is to find out whether and to what extent refugee laws have an impact on the immigration regime discussed in the preceding section, and how the similarities and differences between various refugee laws and practices impact on migration controls.

PRINCIPLES OF INTERNATIONAL REFUGEE LAW

The key global instrument governing refugee matters is the 1951 Convention Relating to the Status of Refugees which, in Africa, is complemented by the 1969 OAU Convention Governing the Specific Aspects of Refugee Problems in Africa. Most countries in the SADC have ratified both instruments.

Under the 1951 UN Convention, a refugee is defined as a person outside his or her country of nationality or habitual residence who has a well-founded fear of persecution for reasons of race, religion, nationality, membership in a particular social group or political opinion.[205] The OAU Convention adopts the above definition and adds that the term "refugee" also applies to every person who is compelled to leave his or her place of habitual residence by external aggression, occu-

pation, foreign domination or events seriously disturbing public order in either part or the whole of the country of origin or nationality.[206] The Conventions exclude any person who has committed a crime against peace, a crime against humanity, a serious non-political crime or who has been guilty of acts contrary to the purposes of the United Nations and, under the 1969 OAU Convention, the purposes of the OAU (now the AU).[207]

The international instruments of refugees, as complemented by human rights treaties, enshrine a number of principles, which have implications for migration controls. The first is the principle of asylum, which ordains that everyone facing persecution has the right to seek asylum in other states.[208] The second is the principle of *non-refoulement*, which provides that a refugee, including an asylum seeker whose status has not been determined, cannot be rejected at the frontier or returned to a country where he or she may face persecution.[209] The legal implication of these two principles is that measures introduced by states for migration control must not have the effect of preventing asylum seekers from accessing, or remaining in, the territories of the states from which they intend to seek asylum. These principles also imply that states must put in place efficient procedures for determining who is a refugee and who is, therefore, entitled to international protection.[210]

In addition, refugee law prohibits states from imposing penalties, on account of illegal entry or presence in the country, on refugees who, coming directly from a territory where they face persecution, enter or are present in their territory without authorization, if they present themselves without delay to the authorities and show good cause for their illegal entry.[211] What this means is that unlike regular migrants, refugees do not need visas/entry permits or any form of prior authorization to enter the territory of a state.

The third is the principle of protection, which guarantees to refugees minimum standards of treatment. Of these standards, those that are most relevant to immigration law are those that relate to matters such as freedom of movement and access to gainful employment.

On movement and residence, Article 26 of the 1951 United Nations Convention on Refugees requires contracting states to accord refugees lawfully in their territories the right to choose their place of residence and to move freely within the territory, subject to any regulations applicable to non-citizens who are generally in the same circumstances.

With regard to gainful employment, states are required by Article 17 to accord to refugees lawfully staying in their territory the most favourable treatment accorded to nationals of a foreign country in the same circumstances. In any case, restrictive measures imposed on foreign citizens for the protection of national

labour markets must not be applied to a refugee who has completed three years of residence in the country, who has a spouse possessing the nationality of the country of residence, or who has one or more children possessing the nationality of the country of residence.

Article 18 requires states to accord a refugee lawfully staying in their territory treatment as favourable as possible. This should be no less favourable than that accorded to non-citizens generally in the same circumstances, with regard to the right to engage in agriculture, industry, handicraft and commerce and to establish commercial and industrial companies. As per Article 19, similar treatment must be accorded to refugees with regard to practising liberal professions.

The other principle is that which enjoins states to find durable solutions to the plight of refugees by way of repatriation, resettlement or local integration. Of these solutions, repatriation is a right of refugees based on, among other norms, the migration-related right of a person to return to his or her own country. While refugees are not as such entitled to local integration, states are required to facilitate their naturalization.

Finally, there is the principle of international co-operation that enjoins states to co-operate in addressing refugee problems. This principle is based on refugee instruments as well as the provisions of the Charter of the United Nations that call upon states to co-operate in resolving problems of humanitarian character.[212]

DEFINING A REFUGEE

There are two main ways by which refugees are defined in various SADC legislation. The first approach, found in more modern legislation, is to provide a specific definition of a refugee normally adopting the same definition of a refugee as that found in the 1951 UN Convention on Refugees and the 1969 OAU Convention on Refugees in Africa. The second, found mainly in legislation enacted in the 1970s, is to simply vest the powers to determine who is a refugee in the minister responsible for refugee affairs.

The acts of legislation that provide for a specific definition of a refugee by adopting the definitions of the term found in the 1951 UN Convention on Refugees and its 1967 protocol, and the 1969 OAU Convention include:

* Angola's *Refugee Status Act*[213]

* Malawi's *Refugee Act*[214]

* Lesotho's *Refugees Act*[215]

- Mozambique's *Refugee Act*[216]
- Namibia's *Refugees (Recognition and Control) Act*[217]
- South Africa's *Refugees Act*[218]
- Tanzania's *Refugees Act*[219]
- Zimbabwe's *Refugees Act*[220]
- Botswana's *Refugees (Recognition and Control) Act*[221]

The Botswana Act provides for a specific definition of a refugee but one that is restricted to the definition of the term under the 1951 UN Convention on Refugees.[222]

Legislation that simply vests the power to determine who is a refugee in the minister includes Swaziland's *Refugees Control Order*[223] and Zambia's *Refugees (Control) Act*.[224] In practice, the bodies that advise the ministers under such Acts are actually guided by the definitions found in international instruments. Indeed, in Zambia, the very first question to be determined when a person applies for asylum is whether the person is basing his or her claim on the 1951 UN Convention or the extended part of the definition of a refugee under the 1969 OAU Convention. Different procedures follow depending on how this question is answered.

All specific definitions of refugees exclude certain persons from being considered. These are normally persons who are excluded from refugee status under the international instruments noted above. However, some legislation extends the list of excludable persons. For example, the Acts of Namibia, Lesotho and Zambia also exclude from refugee status a person who belongs to a category of persons declared by the minister by notice in the Gazette to be not entitled to refugee status.[225]

Under the Tanzanian Act, a person cannot be considered a refugee if, prior to their entry into Tanzania, he or she transited through one or more countries and is unable to show reasonable cause for failure to seek asylum in those countries.[226] South Africa is known to have considered introducing a similar provision.[227] Botswana is also said to consistently reject asylum claims submitted by persons originating from outside the region without looking into the merits of the case.[228] In Zambia, asylum seekers who have transited through safe third countries are presumed, but not conclusively taken, to be economic migrants.

ENTRY INTO AND PRESENCE IN THE COUNTRY OF ASYLUM

In the previous section of this chapter, we noted that the immigration legislation of all SADC countries requires non-citizens to obtain permission to enter the territories of countries of which they are not nationals. While refugee legislation does not remove this requirement as such, it exempts refugees from the consequences of not complying with it. Such exemption is normally found in the provisions relating to *non-refoulement*. Thus, Section 13 of the Zimbabwe Act provides that, "Notwithstanding the provisions of any other law, *no person shall be refused entry into Zimbabwe, expelled, extradited or returned from Zimbabwe* to any other country or be subjected to similar measures if, as a result of such refusal, expulsion, return or other measure, such a person is compelled to return to or remain in a country where...[he or she may face persecution]" (italics added). Other legislation with identical provisions on *non-refoulement* includes the Acts of Angola, Lesotho, Malawi, Mozambique, Namibia, and South Africa.[229]

Under the Botswana Act, the principle of *non-refoulement* applies only to recognised refugees and only if their removal from Botswana will result in threat to their life or freedom on account of their race, religion, nationality or membership in a particular social group. Strictly speaking, this provision does not apply to asylum seekers whose status is yet to be determined or refugees who fall under the extended definition of the OAU Convention.

Under the Tanzanian Act, the only provision that refers to *non-refoulement* is Section 28(4), which prohibits the deportation of an asylum seeker or a refugee to a place where he or she will be tried or punished for an offence of a political character. However, this provision does not fully reflect the provisions of international instruments of *non-refoulement*. First, the section binds only the minister and the courts and only when they are considering making an order of deportation. It does not apply to other officials such as immigration officers who may encounter asylum seekers at the border for example. Secondly, the section protects only those refugees who are facing prosecution or punishment for offences of a political nature. Therefore, refugees facing persecution on other grounds are not protected by this provision.[230] The legislation of Swaziland and Zambia contains no provision of *non-refoulement*. In practice however, this norm is observed.

In addition to general provisions of *non-refoulement* some legislation provides more directly for the right of asylum seekers to enter and remain in countries of asylum. A good example is Section 10(2) of Malawi's Act which provides that *"a person claiming to be a refugee shall be permitted to enter and remain in Malawi..."* until his or her application has been considered (italics added). Under

Section 10(3) of the same Act, even a person who wishes to enter Malawi "for the purposes of proceeding to another country where he intends to seek asylum as a refugee... shall be allowed entry in Malawi" upon such conditions determined by the authorities. In Mozambique and South Africa an asylum seeker must by law be given a provisional residence permit by the authority to which the application is made.[231] Logically, entitlement to temporary residence implies the right of entry. Equally, Section 5(2)(e) of the Tanzanian Act imposes the responsibility on the Director of Refugee Services "to ensure that an applicant for refugee status is not ordered to leave the country before his claim for refugee status has been decided upon." The Namibian Act also provides under Section 14(1) that every person who has applied for asylum as well as any member of their family has a right to remain in Namibia until asylum has been determined.

Much SADC national refugee legislation expressly protects asylum seekers from being penalised for illegal entry or presence. Thus, Section 21(4) of the South African Act provides expressly that, notwithstanding any law to the contrary, no proceedings with respect to illegal entry or presence within the Republic may be instituted or continued against any person who has applied for asylum. Equally, the legislation of Lesotho and Zimbabwe expressly states that the provisions of immigration legislation that imposes penalties for illegal entry or residence do not apply to asylum seekers.[232] A similar provision is found under Section 5 of the Angolan Act.

Under Section 11 of Mozambique's Act, when a person who has been charged with any criminal or administrative offence directly connected with illegal entry into the Republic presents a petition for asylum, such proceedings shall be suspended immediately upon the petition being presented. In other words, in Mozambique, an application for asylum has only suspensive effect. The legislation of Swaziland, Tanzania and Zambia are silent on exemption of asylum seekers from penalties for illegal entry or presence. In Zambia, some asylum seekers have been detained pending determination of their status. The Acts of Angola, Botswana, Namibia, South Africa and Zimbabwe expressly give recognised refugees the right to remain and reside in the country.

Under Section 12 of the Tanzanian Act, a refugee, even after being recognised, must still obtain a permit in order to reside in the country. An authorised officer cannot deny a refugee a resident permit if they have reason to believe that the refusal of a permit will necessitate the return of the refugee to the territory from which they entered Tanzania and in which they will be tried or punished for an offence of a political character or persecuted. However, the section permits the authorised officer to deny any refugee a residence permit upon assigning reasons. These reasons are not specified.

The laws of Swaziland and Zambia do not contain provisions on the right to residence of refugees. On the contrary, the law allows the relevant minister to order, at any time, any refugee to return by such means or route to the territory from which he or she entered the country of asylum.[234] Of course, the practice is different as these countries observe the *non-refoulement* norm.

ASYLUM PROCEDURES

There is no prescribed procedure under international refugee law for refugee status determination. However, in practice, there are two main procedures that are employed for this purpose. The first is group determination whereby a group of asylum seekers is recognised as being composed of refugees on a *prima facie* basis in light of the circumstances that led to their departure from the country of origin.[235] The second is by examining each claimant to determine whether or not he or she is indeed a refugee. Some refugee legislation in SADC makes provision for both procedures.

Prima Facie Status Determination

The typical way the *prima facie* procedure is provided for is by empowering a specified authority, normally the minister responsible for refugee affairs, to declare any class of persons to be refugees under any applicable definition. Where such a declaration is made, it is conclusive as to the status of all members of the class of persons so declared. The countries whose legislation have such a provision are Lesotho, South Africa, Swaziland, Tanzania, Zambia and Zimbabwe.[236]

Under the Malawi Act, the minister appears to be empowered, not to declare a class of persons to be refugees, but to direct the Refugee Committee to consider, on a group basis, the status of any specified group of foreign nationals seeking refugee status in Malawi. Although not expressly provided for under the Refugee Act, this approach is also taken in Tanzania with regard to refugees from Burundi and the DRC.

Individual Status Determination

Individualised procedures for status determination are found under the laws of Angola, Botswana, Namibia, Lesotho, Malawi, Mozambique, South Africa,

Tanzania and Zimbabwe. Such a procedure also exists in Zambia where it has been instituted administratively. In some countries, the procedure is wholly or mainly administrative while in others it is quasi-judicial. A procedure is described as administrative if all or most stages of decision-making are staffed by civil servants and the executive. A procedure is quasi-judicial if there is a substantial involvement of adjudicative bodies that have sufficient independence from the executive.

In virtually all countries, a person who wishes to be recognized as a refugee must present him- or herself to specified government authorities in the area of entry and indicate his or her desire to apply for asylum. Such authorities, if not authorized to deal with asylum matters, will put the asylum seeker in touch with an officer authorized to do so. In South Africa, such an officer, who is known as a Refugee Reception Officer, must issue the asylum seeker with an asylum seeker permit and instruct them to appear before a Refugee Status Determination Officer for an interview on the date specified. After hearing the asylum seeker, the Refugee Status Determination Officer may accept or reject the application. In the case of acceptance, the officer must provide the applicant with written acknowledgement of refugee status.

In Zambia, the first person to deal with individual asylum claims is a legal officer in the office of the Commissioner for Refugees who gives a preliminary interview to the applicant. If, after such interview, the legal officer forms an opinion that the applicant falls under the provisions of the extended definition of a refugee under the OAU Convention, he or she shall immediately recommend to the Refugee Commissioner that refugee status be granted. If the legal officer forms an opinion that the claim falls under the 1951 UN Convention or falls under the OAU Convention but is unfounded, he or she must refer the application to the inter-ministerial committee for determination.

In all other countries, the authorized officer to whom an asylum claim has been presented must take the necessary steps to bring the case before a body competent to examine and determine the asylum claim. The body charged to hear applications for asylum is an inter-ministerial committee typically drawing membership from the departments of refugees, immigration, police and security; the Ministry of Foreign Affairs and the Officer of the President. In a few countries, the Ministries of Education, Labour and Social Affairs are also represented. UNHCR is also represented in an observer capacity.

In Angola and Malawi the committee, after hearing the applicant, can grant refugee status or reject the application.[237] In the rest of the countries, the committee, after hearing the application, recommends whether or not refugee status should be granted. In Namibia and Zimbabwe, such recommendation is made to the commissioner, who makes the decision.[238] In Botswana, Mozambique, Lesotho, Tanzania and Zambia, the recommendation goes to the minister who makes the decision whether or not to grant asylum.[239]

With regard to appeals and reviews, the procedures to be followed depend on the level at which the first instance decision is made and whether or not the procedure followed is administrative or quasi-judicial. Under the Angolan Act, the decision of the Committee appears to be final. In Botswana, Malawi, Tanzania, Zambia and Zimbabwe, appeals are to the Minister, whose decision is final.[240]

In South Africa, an applicant whose application has been rejected must be provided with reasons in writing. If an application is rejected as manifestly unfounded, abusive or fraudulent, then it must be forwarded to the Standing Committee for review. The Standing Committee is constituted by the Chairman, and such other members as the Minister may determine. Appointment is on the basis of experience, expertise and competence. At least one member must be legally qualified.

After such review, the committee may confirm or set aside the decision and send the application back to the Refugee Status Determination Officer with direction for further action. If the application is rejected on any other ground, then the appeal lies with the Appeals Board. The Board is constituted of the Chairman and two other members all appointed by the minister on the basis of their experience, expertise and competence. At least one member must be legally qualified. After hearing the appeal, the Board may confirm, set aside or substitute any decision made by a Refugee Status Determination Officer.

In Namibia, appeals against the decision of the commissioner, including those on status, go to the Refugee Appeals Board. This Board consists of three members appointed by the Minister for Refugee Affairs in consultation with the Minister of Justice. Members must be legal practitioners who possess the necessary knowledge in law.[241]

In Lesotho, an unsuccessful applicant has a "right to re-apply" to the Minister to reconsider his or her application and the Minister may, at their discretion on recommendation by the committee, refer the matter to the Refugee Advisory Board. The Board is appointed by the Minister and is composed of a Chairman, who must be a senior legal practitioner and who is not an employee of the Government; one member of the Interministerial Committee for the Determination of Refugee Status; one member of the Refugee Co-ordination Unit; and a representative of UNHCR in Lesotho as an adviser. The recommendation of the Board is not binding on the Minister. However, if after reconsideration of the applicant's case, the Minister decides to reject the recommendation of the committee, or as the case may be, the Board, the applicant has a right to seek "an appropriate relief" from the High Court of the Kingdom of Lesotho.[242]

In Mozambique, appeals against the ruling of the Minister of the Interior go to the Administrative Court.[243]

IDENTITY AND TRAVEL DOCUMENTS

A number of laws make provisions for granting refugees identity and travel documents. These include Angola, Mozambique, South Africa, Swaziland, Zambia and Zimbabwe. The details required on identity cards differ. Under the Angolan Act, the identity documents must legally accredit the status of refugees as permanent residents. In Zambia and Swaziland, the identity card has to contain "such particulars as may be specified." The Mozambican Act requires that the identity document attest to the refugee status of the holder. The South African Act is more detailed, requiring an identity document issued to a refugee to contain an identity number; the holder's name, full forenames, gender, date of birth and the place or country of birth; the country of citizenship; a recent photograph; and the holder's fingerprints or other prints. Most provisions on travel documents require them to conform to the Specimen Travel Document annexed to the 1951 Convention on Refugees. In Mozambique, more details on travel documents for refugees are found under Articles 53 and 54 of the Immigration Act of 1993.

CONDITIONS OF SOJOURN

Freedom of Movement

There is considerable difference in the laws and practices of various countries with regard to freedom of movement by refugees. Malawi, Tanzania and Zambia entered reservations on Article 26 of the 1951 Convention and their legislation requires refugees to reside in designated areas. This is also the case in Namibia, Swaziland and Zimbabwe. Most of these countries, in practice, require refugees to reside in specified refugee settlements. Refugees are not allowed to leave these settlements without permits unless they have expressly been exempted.[245] In Zambia, under an arrangement agreed with UNHCR, refugees allowed to leave the camps are those awaiting resettlement, facing security threats in camps, professionals with work permits, business persons, students/pupils in Zambian schools and, exceptionally, those refugees falling under the 1951 Convention on Refugees.

By contrast, the South African Act accords recognised refugees full legal protection, which includes the rights set out in Chapter 2 of the Constitution.[246] However, in situations of mass influx, the Minister may, after consultation with UNHCR, designate areas, centres or places for the temporary residence of asylum seekers or refugees.[247] The Botswana Act does not seem to restrict the movement of refugees except those liable to removal from the country.[248]

The legislation of Angola, Lesotho and Mozambique is not explicit about the freedom of movement of refugees. However, this right may be implied from the provisions of the legislation of these countries which grants recognised refugees resident status and the attendant rights and/or those which accord refugees the enjoyment of all the rights under the 1951 UN Convention on refugees.[249]

Wage-Earning Employment

Here too, the laws and practices of SADC countries differ. Under the legislation of Angola and South Africa recognition as a refugee automatically entitles a person to engage in gainful activities.[250] In Angola, the right to work applies even to asylum seekers whose cases are still under consideration. However, in South Africa, the asylum seeker's permit expressly excludes the right to work. In Mozambique, the right to engage in economic activities would presumably flow from the resident status that, as seen above, refugees enjoy in the country.

By contrast, under Section 32 of the Tanzanian Refugees Act a refugee, even after being recognised and granted asylum, must first obtain a work permit in order to engage in any economic activity. This application must be made to the Director for Refugee Services, who may issue the permit after consultations with the ministry responsible for labour. Any refugee who works or engages him or herself in any economic activity without a permit commits an offence under the Act and, upon conviction, is liable to a hefty fine or imprisonment for a period not exceeding three years.

In practice, the Director for Refugee Services does not issue work permits. Instead, their office receives applications for work permits from refugees, and then forwards them to the Immigration Department, which effectively treats them in the same way as any other application for a work permit by a foreigner.

In Botswana, a recognised refugee appears to require a work permit. This is by virtue of Section 8(3) which provides that, "Except where this Act otherwise provides, a person who is recognised as a political refugee shall be subject to the provisions of Immigration Act in all respects as if the declaration of recognition had not been made." There is no provision in the Act that grants refugees the right

to work. Also, under Section 12(3) of the Zimbabwe Act, refugees are to be treated the same as any person who is not a citizen of Zimbabwe with regard to engagement in wage-earning employment. This implies that they need a permit to work. In practice that is the case.

The legislation of Malawi and Zambia is silent on the issue of engagement by refugees in gainful employment. However, Malawi entered reservations on the relevant provisions of the 1951 Convention.[251] In the past, both these countries used to liberally allow refugees to seek employment or establish their own businesses. Currently, however, both countries require refugees who wish to engage in economic activities to apply for permits like any other foreigner. Both countries will issue work permits to refugees for work in areas where there is a skills shortage. Applicants must complete all the normal application forms, present evidence of their qualifications and pay the necessary fees. Since the closure of the urban refugee programme and the removal of all refugees to rural settlements, refugees wishing to work in Zimbabwe must obtain a work permit. The main reason given for imposing these restrictions is said to be the protection of the local labour market.

In Zambia, the requirement that refugees obtain work permits was imposed after it was realised that the earlier regime, whereby refugees were treated like citizens, was being abused by unscrupulous foreigners who applied for refugee status solely or mainly for the purpose of engaging in economic activities in Zambia.

Durable Solutions: Naturalisation

The legislation of Lesotho, Mozambique and South Africa has provisions that make it possible for refugees to be naturalized those countries. In Lesotho, Section 14 of the Refugees Act allows a refugee to apply for naturalization to the Minister responsible for Interior and Chieftainship Affairs if he or she meets the conditions set out in the Schedule to the Act. The Schedule requires the applicant to have resided in Lesotho throughout the twelve-month period immediately preceding the date of application, and immediately preceding said period he or she must have resided in Lesotho for periods amounting in aggregate to not less than five years. In special circumstances, the Minister may waive this latter requirement. In addition, the applicant must have adequate knowledge of Sesotho or English; be of good character; show that they would be a suitable citizen of Lesotho; and intend, if naturalized, to reside permanently in Lesotho. A refugee whose application for naturalization is successful becomes a citizen of Lesotho by naturalization.

Article 12(1) of the Mozambican Act provides that, "the Republic of Mozambique may authorize the acquisition of Mozambican nationality by naturalization for any person who has refugee status and who seeks to acquire such nationality by that means." Article 12(2) provides further that, "once the requirements of the legislation concerning nationality have been met, naturalization shall be granted on the same terms as to other aliens."

In South Africa, Section 27(c) of the South African Refugees Act entitles a refugee to apply for an immigration permit under the Aliens Control Act of 1991 after five years of continuous residence in the Republic from the date on which he or she was granted asylum, if the Standing Committee certifies that he or she will remain a refugee indefinitely. Having such a permit potentially sets the holder on course to apply for naturalization under the Citizenship Act of 1995.

The Malawi Refugee Act does not address the issue of naturalization. But on acceding to the 1951 Convention on Refugees, Malawi entered a reservation to the provisions relating to, among other things, naturalization and assimilation of refugees.[252] Also silent on naturalization is the Botswana Refugees Act. But under Section 13 of the Act, a refugee residing in Botswana is not regarded as being ordinarily resident in Botswana for the purposes of any written law other than a taxation law. This provision excludes refugees from benefiting *qua* refugees from the provisions of the Botswana Citizenship Act of 1998 under which a person who has been resident for a qualifying period can apply for naturalization.

The refugee acts of Tanzania, Zambia and Zimbabwe are also silent on the question of naturalization. While countries like Tanzania did in the past naturalise thousands of refugees, the policy currently pursued in these three countries is to not allow naturalization via the refugee route. Instead, they have adopted the policy of temporary protection, pending repatriation when conditions in the countries of origin permit. In Zambia and Tanzania, this policy is linked to the huge number of refugees who entered and remained in their territories for a long time. In Zimbabwe, it is thought that naturalization of refugees could necessitate giving them land which may not be easy in a country where many native Zimbabweans remain landless as a result of the colonial legacy.

CONCLUSION

It is clear from the foregoing discussion that refugee law has a significant impact on immigration regulation. All countries under review have ratified international instruments on refugees. However, not all refugee acts have incorporated all the key principles of international instruments on refugee protection. This is particularly so with laws enacted in the 1970s. These acts are much more about controlling refugees than about protecting them. Nevertheless, these laws have been complemented or supplanted by administrative arrangements that have brought practice in those countries in line with acceptable standards.

While there is a degree of uniformity in the way refugee matters are dealt with, there are some differences in law and practice, with implications for migration controls. All countries adopt the definition of a refugee as found in international instruments. However, some qualify this definition especially with regard to who is excluded from refugee status. For example, at least two pieces of legislation empower the minister to declare a class of persons to not be refugees. Some countries exclude from refugee status persons who have transited through a third safe country.

Most legislation exempts refugees from the provisions of immigration laws that require entry permits and penalize illegal entry. Most acts enacted in the 1970s are silent on this matter. In at least one country with such legislation, asylum seekers have sometimes been detained as "illegal migrants" pending the hearing of their claims.

Considerable differences are found in the provisions and practices of the conditions of sojourn. Some countries allow refugees full freedom of movement within the territory of the country of asylum. Others restrict this freedom by requiring refugees to reside in designated areas. A few countries accord refugees the same treatment as permanent residents with regard to engaging in gainful employment, including wage employment. However, the majority of countries treat refugees like other foreigners, requiring them to obtain work permits before they can work.

Very few countries allow refugees to apply for naturalization. Indeed, many do not consider residence as a refugee as a route towards acquiring citizenship by naturalization.

Differential treatment of refugees by various countries may not necessarily be wrong, especially if it does not result in breach of international norms of refugee protection. However, such differences can have an impact on migration management, particularly in countries under regionalizing schemes such as SADC. For example, the application of the safe third country rule can have the impact of confining refugees in the countries immediately bordering the countries of origin.

Differences in asylum application procedures and standards of treatment are known to contribute to the phenomenon of irregular movement of asylum seekers and refugees. This is acknowledged in paragraph (b) of EXCOM Conclusion No

58 (XL) on the problem of irregular movement of refugees which states: "irregular movements of refugees and asylum-seekers who have already found protection in a country are, to a large extent, composed of persons who feel impelled to leave, due to the absence of educational and employment possibilities and the non-availability of long-term durable solutions by way of voluntary repartition, local integration and resettlement."

In various countries we visited, we were told of refugees who would move on to other SADC countries even after they had been given asylum. The countries to which refugees tend to move suggest that better treatment and opportunities are the reasons for secondary movements.

6 RECOMMENDATION:

The final chapter of this report contains various conclusions and recommendations coming out of the foregoing analysis. It should be emphasized that these are the opinions and recommendations of the authors of the report and do not represent the official position of the Southern African Migration Project (SAMP), the International Organisation for Migration (IOM) or any of the other MIDSA partners. Nor do they represent the views of the funders of this project, the Canadian International Development Agency (CIDA) and the US Bureau for Population, Refugees and Migration. They are presented here as a stimulus to debate about the desirability and possibility of harmonization of immigration-related laws across the SADC.

The recommendations in this chapter are made to the participating countries in MIDSA. Since these countries are co-terminous with SADC, the recommendations will, we hope, also be of interest to the SADC and be taken up at the ministerial level.

Recommendations with regard to citizenship are particularly difficult to make from a regional perspective, since citizenship policy is closely linked to a country's sovereignty. However, there are some places where the laws of citizenship interact in such a way as to create a problem of citizenship that stretches across borders.

One such instance is the group of persons resident for many years in Namibia who remain nationals of Angola and other countries. Indeed, there are several groups of potential citizens in Namibia who are precluded from citizenship in terms of Namibian law in part because of the non-renunciation policies of their countries of origin, such as Angola. It is likely that these groups are disproportionately composed of women. This issue (the interaction of acquisition and renunciation policies) is a site for legal reform investigation and potential harmonization. Some of the potential solutions worth investigation are the option of adopting a policy of renunciation in the country of origin (Angola) and the option of the country of naturalization (Namibia) adopting a more flexible policy towards the renunciation requirement such as exists in Tanzania.

A second recommendation focuses on gender concerns. With respect to renunciation, with respect to marriage/naturalization, and with respect to marriages of convenience (discussed also in Chapter 4), it is apparent that substantial changes in the citizenship regime are linked to the changing roles and position of women in Southern Africa. Indeed, citizenship policy often impacts dramatically and negatively on women.

Given the close identification of permanent residents with citizenship in some but not all the countries of SADC and given the increasing use made of citizenship status as a policy tool, a comparison of the substantive rights of these persons will be of use to policy-makers. A survey on this topic will also be of use in evaluating the policies of national identification documents.

Recommendation No. 1: An investigation should be launched of the interaction of acquisition and renunciation of citizenship policies.

Recommendation No. 2: An examination should be made of bilateral gendered migration among member countries with respect to citizenship with a view towards developing model procedures of renunciation and acquisition of citizenship by marriage that aim to reduce the vulnerability of women and children.

Recommendation No. 3: A country-by-country survey of the social and economic rights of permanent residents as opposed to citizens should be undertaken in regards to matters such as health care, municipal services, and social security.

The ultimate objective of a system of population registration and identification should be to ensure the accuracy, reliability and retrievability of information in registers. There is a strong case for harmonization of these procedures across the SADC region. The following recommendations are intended to improve the quality of registration and identification laws including the accuracy, reliability and retrievability of information in registers as well as their role in facilitating the fashioning of a regional immigration regime in SADC. Some of these recommendations are based on the "best practices" observed during the research in some SADC states.

Recommendation No. 4: All relevant legislation pertaining to population registration and identification should be harmonized.

Recommendation No. 5: General registration and identification of persons should be compulsory to all in all jurisdictions and measures should be taken to ensure all persons, particularly the rural poor, have access to registration facilities. In this regard, mobile registration units should be introduced to service people in remote areas and education campaigns should be conducted on the importance of population registration. In addition, certificates and identity documents made on the basis of information in registers must be considered to be sufficient evidence of the contents, unless and until evidence to the contrary is provided.

Recommendation No. 6: Governments should commit sufficient resources to ensure efficient administration of the registration and identification systems. In particular, all governments should endeavour to computerise their records to ensure security and ease of retrieving the records. All registers must be centralised as far as is possible.

In order to exploit the potential of registers in facilitating regional mobility, SADC countries could explore the possibility of putting certain particulars in the population register on a shareable computerised record. This can facilitate the identification of SADC citizens wherever they happen to be in the region, which in turn should ease the restrictions on movement within the region. Such an arrangement exists between Australia and New Zealand. Consequently, New Zealanders are the only persons who do not need visas to go to Australia and vice versa.

Recommendation No. 7: Particulars in the population register of each country should be placed on a shareable computerised data base.

There is also a strong case for a similar approach to legislation relating to registration of births and deaths.

Recommendation No. 8: All laws and procedures relating to registration of births and deaths should be reviewed and harmonized to ensure that all legislation has all the basic elements of a sound system for such registration. Registration of births and deaths should be made compulsory for all in all countries.

Recommendation No. 9: Measures should be put in place to ensure that all persons, particularly the rural poor, participate fully in the system of registration of births and deaths. To achieve this registration offices must be placed as close as possible to the people. One of the steps that could be taken in this regard is the establishment of as many registration offices as is financially feasible.

A good example of improving accessibility is Mauritius where some forty-six Civil Status Sub-Offices have been established to service a population of 1.2 million people.[253] Where this is not feasible, governments may explore the utilisation of the lowest levels of local and central government in the collection, recording and reporting information required for registration of births and deaths. As was seen above, laws such as those of Lesotho and Swaziland already seem to provide for this and could be emulated by others.

The provisions of the laws, as well as the administrative arrangements put in place for the implementation of registration of births and deaths should ideally be geared towards ensuring the accuracy of the records and preventing tampering with the same. Consequently, certificates and identity documents made on the basis of information in registers must be considered to be sufficient evidence of the contents, unless and until evidence to the contrary is provided.

Recommendation No. 10: Governments should commit sufficient resources to ensure efficient administration of the registration of births and deaths. In particular, all governments should endeavour to computerise their records to ensure security and ease of retrieving the records. All registers should be centralised as far as is possible.

As shown in the Introduction and the SADC Protocols sections of the Immigration chapter, there are a number of international instruments and agreements relevant to the national migration regimes of the SADC countries. Apart from the refugee conventions, most of the agreements that have been concluded by SADC countries are operational and technical. Additionally, there are the bilateral agreements between South Africa and its neighbouring countries that cover the policy areas of labour and repatriation. To this point, these agreements have been approached in a bilateral fashion.

With respect to the border security, inter-agency cooperation and the operational area, MIDSA would seem to be well-positioned to further investigate and report on SADC region best practice. A number of areas bear investigation including the relative merits of border posts versus country-to-country agreements and the inclusion of security forces beyond the immigration authorities within such operation structures. Although the grounds of exclusion of the SADC countries have been shown to be largely harmonized, this investigation into the operational policy area may directly lead to better border security and immigration regulation.

Recommendation No. 11: An investigation should be made of regional and international best practice with respect to procedures of exclusion and expulsion and border security and with respect to sharing of this practice within SADC.

With respect to repatriation regulation, country interests within SADC are likely to be somewhat divergent. Nonetheless, this is an area that is increas-

ingly being regulated internationally with the conclusion of regional agreements. Such agreements can also provide for respect of human rights (some of which issues are complex and go beyond refugee-related concerns) while also sharing the burden of repatriation costs.[254]

Recommendation No. 12: It is recommended that a model repatriation agreement be drafted to serve between SADC countries. Although such a model agreement would be a starting point for bilateral negotiation, it could facilitate harmonization by at least ensuring that a common set of legal concepts are used and a common set of policy issues are addressed.

Recommendation No. 13: A second model repatriation agreement should be drafted for use by SADC countries with non–SADC countries.

Again, such a model agreement would provide a mere template for bilateral negotiation. However, it would ensure that repatriation policies of the SADC countries with foreign states outside the SADC region could be safeguarded against inconsistencies and loopholes which unauthorized migrants could exploit.

In light of the joint repatriation and labour conditions regulation nature of the currently existing bilateral labour agreements, it is suggested that the existing agreements be comprehensively evaluated and a model labour migration agreement be drawn up. This model agreement should point in several directions: (a) fit within international law and best practice as applied to the SADC region, (b) put into place appropriate domestic and SADC–level mechanisms to monitor the implementation of the agreements, (c) ensure that the procedures of the labour migration agreement are consistent with those of the repatriation model agreements, (d) reduce the opportunities for abuse and violation of human rights of migrants in particular with respect to rights of family life and social security and the issue of compulsory deferred pay, and (e) ensure that burdens of enforcement costs are shared.

Recommendation No. 14: A new model bilateral agreement for labour migration between SADC countries should be drafted.

The third category of agreements overlaps to some extent with existing SADC protocols and initiatives such as labour movement within the education sector or the explorations with respect to General Agreement on Trade in Services. Here, there are two needs. The first is to implement those provisions of existing SADC protocols bearing on migration. This must be done through national legislation, using national as well as SADC processes. The second need is to allow the expertise of the immigration authorities to inform SADC debates concerning the adoption of further protocols.

Recommendation No. 15: It is recommended that MIDSA have a regular item on its agenda to report on the status of immigration-relevant SADC protocols.

There are also a number of legal issues that do not fall within the purview of either international or regional instruments. Nonetheless, harmonization of these policy provisions is worth pursuing. There are at least two specific areas identified in this report. Each of these areas is identified together with a recommended way forward, e.g., either a model agreement to be adapted (where the legal issues are complex or significant) or national investigation (where the legal issues are not so complex but are more tied in with general management and budgetary issues).

With regard to offences and penalties, SADC countries might investigate the creation of an anti-trafficking offence.[255] One way to do this is through the development of a model anti-trafficking provision, which would of course need to be adapted to each national legislative regime. It will, however, be crucial to involve human rights concerns in any such investigation. Given the impact of trafficking on women and their participation in this practice, it will be equally crucial to involve those from this community.

Recommendation No. 16: All SADC countries should create an anti-trafficking offence at the earliest opportunity.

Countries could also investigate the possibility of designating some of their migration offences as administrative offences, punishable by a fine only. One way to do this would be through national investigation in the context of an overall review of management and finances.

Recommendation No. 17: All SADC countries should investigate the possibility of designating some of their migration offences as administrative offences.

The matter of marriages of convenience had become a crucial one for migration regimes in SADC. So too is the immigration status (and practices) of partners accompanying permit-holders in various categories of temporary residence including temporary employment.

Recommendation No. 18: It is recommended that a MIDSA technical workshop be convened with regard to the regulation of marriages of convenience. Furthermore, such a workshop should include participation of SADC persons or organizations with gender expertise as well as persons or organizations with migration expertise.

One recommendation to the organizers of MIDSA is that a topic be proposed to the MIDSA partners regarding financial aspects of migration management. This topic could cover the success of the privatization model employed by South Africa, the use of carrier sanctions and fees-for-services, and the costs of specialist government agencies within labour migration regulation.

Recommendation No. 19: It is recommended that MIDSA consider a workshop on the issue of financial and budgeting aspects of migration management.

Underlying these and other proposals is a recommendation regarding the status of MIDSA itself. This report demonstrates that the present is a time of intense legislative interest and change in the migration regimes of the SADC countries. The debate over the Free Movement Protocol underlines rather than diminishes this point. At such a time, it is unfortunate that there is no SADC focal point regarding migration.

Recommendation No. 20: It is recommended that SADC develop a focal point for migration issues in the community.

A key prerequisite for the implementation of the recommendations of this report is that a SADC–wide facilitated legal drafting process be initiated.[256] In the light of the information presented in this report, there are likely to be some provisions in the immigration laws of each country that require investigation and may well need to be redrafted. Clearly, such a process of legal revision will happen at national level and cannot be usefully driven or coordinated at a regional level. However, that process can be facilitated at a SADC level.

This facilitation of legal revision can occur in two ways. First, there are some substantive provisions of SADC law that can be inserted into national legislation. Some of these provisions have been identified above and include: (1) a uniform visa entry document for tourists to be implemented at the SADC level, following from the SADC protocol on tourism and (2) that immigration formalities regarding education migration in SADC be harmonized as per the SADC Protocol on Education and Training. It would be most effective to pursue this SADC implementation in a regional process.

MIDSA could also play a key role in this process. For instance, where a MIDSA event in a particular policy area includes significant regional participation, MIDSA should attempt to include as part of the material either presented to or placed in front of that event, a survey of current regional legal practice with respect to that policy area.

Second, there are a number of good legal ideas that are worth examining within the region. The most compelling of these depart from an economic rationale. While some of these lend themselves to a model clause or model provision approach, some do not. In the first category, since national experience with investor permits is just beginning, it is worth working with the trade departments of the region to assess the adequacy of legal forms of these permits in light of implementation and enforcement capacity. In this investigation, SADC should urgently investigate the national immigration vehicles towards and barriers to compliance with a SADC regional framework consistent with the General

Agreement on Trade in Services. In the second category, the SADC legal secretariat could develop a model clause and negotiate a treaty permit category in national legislation. Such a SADC treaty permit would be one that its officials may make immediate use of but which may also serve as a legal vehicle for implementation of further bilateral and multilateral movement liberalization.

In the pursuit of national legal reform generally, it would be cost-effective to pursue these implementing legal reform measures drawing upon SADC-wide expertise. One way in which this might happen would be for each country to nominate an official or other person with legal reform drafting and expertise. For greatest effectiveness, this person should be nominated within the line function department. In most cases, this will be the department of immigration. This nominated country representative could participate in an annual series of education and drafting workshops coordinated at the MIDSA level. This nominated country representative would work with the national institutions in the period of time between the annual workshops. A secondary goal of this recommendation would be capacity-building for the nominated country representative. Ideally, such a process would be put into place over a three- to five-year time span.

Three concrete measures could be taken in order to minimise the actual and potential negative consequences of the disparities in refugee legislation within SADC.

Ratification of International Instruments and Revision of Legislation

SADC countries that may have not ratified international instruments on refugees should do so. Those who did so with reservations on economic and social rights should consider lifting them. Countries whose legislation is not compatible with international instruments should consider updating them. It is noteworthy in this regard that Zambia and Malawi are already taking measures in this regard.

Harmonisation of Procedures and Standards of Treatment

SADC states should review their procedures to ensure that they are fair and efficient. They should also harmonise the standards of treatment for asylum seekers and refugees. This can be achieved through joint standard setting with regard to core rights of refugees such as movement, food, shelter, education, and employment and harmonisation of related practices. A forum like MIDSA can play a key role in this regard.

By harmonisation of standards of treatment, it is not suggested here that the treatment of refugees in these matters must be exactly the same in all countries. This will inevitably depend on factors peculiar to each host country including the nature and magnitude of the refugee problem and the economic capacity of the state. What we mean is that minimum standards must be set which should be enjoyed by all refugees irrespective of where in the region they happen to be. States that are unable to meet such standards should be assisted by other SADC states through the mechanisms of burden sharing.

With regard to freedom of movement it is recommended that refugees should only be compelled to live in designated areas in exceptional circumstances such as mass influxes and where such a measure is necessary to safeguard the security of the host country or that of refugees themselves. Otherwise refugees should enjoy freedom of movement.

In relation to gainful employment, SADC countries should allow refugees to engage in economic activities except where doing so seriously threatens the local labour market. Also, host states, in collaboration with UNHCR and other aid agencies, must ensure that each refugee receives recommended food rations and enjoys the minimum standards of shelter as recommended by competent organisations

While a general right to seek naturalisation may not be feasible in countries with huge numbers of refugees and in which the refugee problem is chronic, this solution should not be completely ruled out. To some refugees, this may be the only durable solution feasible for them.

Intra-SADC Co-operation and Burden-Sharing

It is now generally agreed that the best way to deal with forced migration is to take joint steps to address its root causes as well as the consequences of this phenomenon.[257] This approach is already endorsed by SADC. In July 1996, SADC signed a Memorandum of Understanding with the UNHCR whose Article IV enjoins SADC and UNHCR, among other things, to:

1. Address the social, economic, and political issues in the region, particularly those which have a bearing on the root causes of forced population displacement, refugee protection, provision of humanitarian assistance and the search for durable solutions.

2. Establish or strengthen mechanisms, procedures and institutions at national, regional and international levels, in order to create sustainable local capacity for the provision of protection and assistance to refugees and to give effect to the concept of burden sharing.

At its meeting in Maputo, Republic of Mozambique, between 28 and 29 January 1998, the SADC Council of Ministers reviewed the problem of refugees in the region and noted in particular the arrival of refugees from the war-torn Great Lakes region and the implications of their presence for the security of the SADC region. The Ministers reiterated that the cornerstone of SADC was the need to support the most vulnerable peoples though regional integration based in the promotion of democracy, good governance and the respect for human rights. The Council also recognised that preventive measures are not a substitute but a complement to protective measures by reaffirming its awareness of the need for establishing a regional mechanism for safeguarding the human rights of refugees.

As a practical measure to implement a comprehensive regional approach to the problem of refugees in the SADC region, the Council urged Member States to adopt measures towards the harmonisation and unification of procedures and criteria for the protection and provisions of social support of refugees. The Council also set up a working group of nine countries which it directed to come up with proposals on how best the problems of refugees could be addressed in the SADC region and to draw up a Declaration on Refugees for consideration by the Summit of SADC. However, this project seems not to have come to fruition. The SADC countries should consider reviving this initiative.

NOTES

1   Even scholars primarily interested in state consolidation have examined the cultural ways in which citizenship laws may contribute. See J Herbst *States and Power in Africa: Comparative Lessons in Authority and Control* (Princeton NJ: Princeton University Press, 2000) 227-247 (arguing that citizenship has a greater salience than ethnic ties across borders).
2   For a brief history of South African citizenship from 1949 to 1995 see J Klaaren 'Post-Apartheid Citizenship in South Africa' in T Aleinikoff and D Klusmeyer (eds) *From Migrants to Citizens: Membership in a Changing World* (Washington DC: Carnegie Endowment for International Peace, 2000) 221-252.
3   In this report, the terms "nationality" and "citizenship" are used interchangeably. Often, nationality is used at the level of international law and citizenship used at the level of domestic or national law.
4   Act 2 of 1982 (6 April 1982) (UNHCR translation).
5   Section XX of the Immigration Chapter compares the rights and status of citizens and the rights and status of permanent residents in the SADC countries.
6   For this and the preceding paragraph, see T Aleinikoff and D Klusmeyer 'Plural Nationality: Facing the Future in a Migratory World' in T Aleinikoff and D Klusmeyer (eds) *Citizenship Today: Global Perspectives and Practices* (Washington DC: Carnegie Endowment for International Peace, 2001) 63-88.

7   Within the migration sector, these rules as detailed in Table 18 are regarded as Constitutional in status.

8   The Tanzanian legislation is a consolidation of earlier legislation.

9   Botswana's 1998 citizenship legislation differs only marginally from its 1982 legislation.

10 See J Klaaren 'Post-Apartheid Citizenship in South Africa' in Aleinikoff and Klusmeyer (eds) *From Migrants to Citizens*: 221-252. There may, however, be changes to South Africa's citizenship regime in the Immigration Act 13 of 2002 which prevails over the Citizenship Act in the event of inconsistency.

11 This table is based on the first three columns of Table 3-1 contained in T Aleinikoff and D Klusmeyer 'Plural Nationality: Facing the Future in a Migratory World' 66-68.

12 For one discussion of the legal traditions within SADC, see A Thomashausen 'The Enforcement and Recognition of Judgments and Other Forms of Legal Cooperation in the SADC' *Comparative and International Law of South Africa* 35 (2002) 26-37 (suggesting EU experience could be helpful for SADC harmonization).

13 Mauritius had the right of *jus soli* until 1 September 1995.

14 The Seychelles may do this as well.

15 As Table 3 notes, naturalization is referred to as "registration" in Swaziland, Zambia, and Zimbabwe. Naturalization can be roughly defined as the acquisition of citizenship by a route other than territorial birth, descent, marriage, or linkage to former citizenship.

16 The only explicit mention of authority for such a requirement is in s 10(d) of the Swaziland Citizenship Act, giving failure to renounce upon being required to do so as a possible ground for deprivation of Swazi citizenship.

17 The proposal for a new immigration and citizenship regime in Lesotho includes the proposal that naturalizing citizens speak both English and Sesotho.

18 Swaziland has this concern as a grounds for deprivation of citizenship with respect to women.

19 Three of the SADC countries do not use the terminology of citizenship by registration at all: South Africa, Swaziland, and Tanzania. Since we have not discussed adoption and acquisition of citizenship by minor children in the section on the right to citizenship by naturalization, we discuss those topics here in relation to South Africa and Tanzania, even though the formal term those countries use is "naturalization."

20 Mozambique has probably the most radical independence break in its citizenship regime of these SADC countries.

21 Zambia appears to be the exception here.

22 For an account of the legislative history of the 1995 South African Citizenship Act including a discussion of this 1993 Act see Klaaren 'Post-Apartheid Citizenship in South Africa'

23 Some SADC countries use their citizenship laws to declare their citizens to be citizens of the Commonwealth. See for instance s 19 of Botswana's Act: "Every person who is a citizen of Botswana or any Commonwealth country shall, by virtue of that citizenship, also have the status of a Commonwealth citizen."

24 See s 2(4)(a) (if born in Republic and adopted, then citizen by birth) and s 3(1)(b)(iii) (if born outside Republic and then adopted, citizen by descent).

25 While they may be formally gender neutral, laws that mandate loss of citizenship upon marriage in practice impact more substantially on women than on men.

26 In some countries such as Namibia and South Africa, a distinction is drawn between deprivation of citizenship and loss of citizenship. The difference is in the procedure. Loss of citizenship is automatic; deprivation is by ministerial order. We will combine these two procedures here.

27 Swaziland is an exception and has no explicit policy on reacquisition of citizenship.

28 Historically, reacquisition was also important for persons who gave up their citizenship at independence but have since wished to reacquire that citizenship. See also

the Zimbabwean exclusion of voluntary renunciation as a revocable ground for reacquisition of citizenship.

29 This procedure is common within the British legal tradition but is not apparent in the Mozambican law.

30 M Feldblum 'Managing Membership: New Trends in Citizenship and Nationality Policy' in Aleinikoff and Klusmeyer (eds) *From Migrants to Citizens* 475-499.

31 No 26 of 1986 (hereinafter the Botswana Act).

32 Cap 15:02 (hereinafter the Malawi Act).

33 Hereinafter the Lesotho Identification Act.

34 Decree No. 4/99 of 2 March 1999, unofficial translation (hereinafter the Mozambican Decree).

35 No 22 of 1996 (hereinafter the Namibian Identification Act).

36 No 68 of 1997 (hereinafter the South African Identification Act).

37 No 4 of 1998 (hereinafter the Swazi Order).

38 No 4 of 1986 (hereinafter the Tanzanian Act).

39 Cap 126 (hereinafter the Zambian Act).

40 Cap 10:17 (hereinafter the Zimbabwe Act).

41 E.g., Lesotho's, Namibia's, South Africa's, Swaziland's, Tanzania's and Zambia's Act deal with registration and identification separately. The South African Identification Act, section 3; the Swazi Order, section 3(1); the Namibian Identification Act, section 2(1); the Malawi Act, section 5(4) and the Zambian Act, section 3 deal with registration and identification under one statute.

42 Section 6 of the Botswana Act as amended by The National Registration (Amendment) Act, No 17 of 1993.

43 National Registration Act, 1976 (Cap 10:17), section 6.

44 Id. section 6(4).

45 Id. section 2.

46 Zambian Act, section 6.

47 Section 5 of the Aliens (Registration and Status) Act.

48 Section 5 of the South African Identification Act.

49 Section 3(1) read together with section 2; and section 5 of the Zimbabwe Act.

50 Malawi Act, s 4 and Zambian Act, s 4.

51 See s 2 of the Namibian Identification Act.

52 Sections 3(1) and 5(1) of the Botswana and Tanzanian Acts, respectively.

53 See Lesotho's Passports and Identity Card Services Act, s 19.

54 Section 3(2) of the Botswana Act and section 5(2) of the Tanzanian Act.

55 Section 3(3) of the Botswana Act; section 2 of the Swazi Order, section 4 of the South African Identification Act and section 18 of the Namibian Indentification Act.

56 Section 8 of the Tanzanian Act and Zambia's Births and Deaths Registration (General) Rules, rule 5.

57 Lesotho Passports and Identification Card Services Act, s 20.

58 See section 5(2) read in conjunction with section 2.

59 Sections 2(2) and 3(2) of the Namibian Identification Act and Swazi Order, respectively.

60 See the National Registration Form in the First Schedule to Botswana's National Registration Regulations (1987); Namibian Identification Act, section 3; South African Identification Act, sections 8 and 9, Swazi Order, section 4(1) and the Zimbabwe Act, section 6(2).

61 The Zimbabwe Act, section 6(2)(a)(ii).

62 Botswana's Application for Registration Form and the Swazi Oder, section 4(1)(h). South Africa also requires every applicant for registration to furnish particulars of passports and travel documents issued to him or her.

63 Sections 3(f) and 8(i) of the Namibian and South African Identification Acts, and section 4(1)(j) of the Swazi Order, respectively.
64 Section 8 of the South African Identification Act.
65 See South African Act, section 12; Namibian Identification Act, section 9 ; Swazi Order, section 12 and Zambian Act, section 7.
66 See the Botswana Act, s 21; the Namibia Identification Act, s 16; the Tanzanian Act, s 16 and the Zambian Act, s 12.
67 Sections 16 and 18, and 15 of the Lesotho and South African Identification Acts, respectively.
68 See the Botswana Act, s 9(1); Tanzanian Act, s 10(2) and the Zambian Act, s 8(1).
69 Sections 5 and 7 of the Namibian and Swazi Order, respectively.
70 Sections 3(1) and 5(1) of the Botswana and Tanzanian Acts, respectively.
71 Section 3(1) read together with section 2; and section 5 of the Zimbabwe Act.
72 The South African Identification Act, passim and section 5(1) of the Namibian Identification Act.
73 Sections 3(1) and (3) of the Botswana Act; section 2 of the Swazi Order; section 5(1) of the Tanzanian Act; section 4 of the South African Identification Act and section 18 of the Namibian Identification Act.
74 See the Botswana Act, s 9; the Tanzanian Act, s 9(1) ; the Zambian Act, s 3; the Zimbabwe Act, s 7; the Swazi Order s 7(1)(a); the Namibian Act s 5; and the South African Act s 14.
75 Namibian Identification Act, s 5(1) and (2); Swazi Order, s.7(1)(A) and (b); the South African Identification Act, s 15(1) and the Zambian Act, s 3.
76 The Namibian Identification Act, ss 7 and 8; the Swazi Order ss 9 and 10; the South African Identification Act, ss 9 and 10; and the Zambian Act, s 6(2).
77 Section 9(1) of the Botswana Act and section 10(2) of the Tanzanian Act.
78 Namibian Identification Act, section 5(1) and (2); Swazi Order, section 7(1)(A) and (b); and the South African Identification Act, section 15(1).
79 Section 17(2) of the South African Identification Act and section10(2) of the Namibian Identification Act.
80 Section 7 of the Zimbabwe Act.
81 See e.g. The Botswana Act, section 10; the Tanzanian Act, section 10; the Zimbabwe Act, section 7(2) and the South African Identification Act, section 14.
82 See e.g. the Namibian Identification Act, section 5(2) and the Swazi Order, section 6.
83 Article 2 of the Mozambican National Registration Act.
84 See Regulation 3(b)(ii).
85 See e.g. section 17(1) of the South African Identification Act and section 10(1) of the Namibian Act.
86 See J Klaaren and J Ramji 'Inside Illegality: Migration Policing in South Africa after Apartheid' *Africa Today* 48 (2002) 35-47.
87 Section 17(4) of the South African Identification Act.
88 Act No 1 of 2002.
89 The Zambian Act, s 9(2).
90 Sections 10(b) and (c).
91 The Births and Deaths Registration Ordinance (Chapter 108), section 3(2).
92 Chapter 30:1, as amended from time to time.
93 Chapter 24:01, as amended from time to time.
94 Of 1981, as amended from time to time.
95 No 51 of 1992, as amended from time to time.
96 No 5 of 1983, as amended from time to time.
97 Chapter 108 of the Laws, as amended from time to time.
98 Chapter 51 of the Laws of Zambia.

99   Act No 11 of 1986, as amended from time to time.
100 The Malawi Act, section 14; The Tanzania Ordinance, section 3; the Zambian Act, sections 4 and 8; and the Zimbabwe Act, section 3.
101 See the Botswana Act, section 3 and the Swazi Act, section3.
102 Mauritius Act, section 3 and the South Africa's Act, section 3.
103 Mauritius Act, section 12; South African Act, section 9; Swazi Act, sections 15; Zambian Act, section 5 and Zimbabwe Act, section 10.
104 Voluntary and compulsory registration is provided for under parts II and III of the Botswana Act, respectively.
105 Under sections 18 and 25 of the Malawi and Tanzania laws, respectively.
106 See Form B1 of the First Schedule of Botswana's Birth and Deaths Registration Regulations (1969); Form F of Malawi's Births and Deaths Registration (General) Rules (1966); Section 13 of the Mauritius Act; Rule 7 of Tanganyika's Registration of Births and Deaths Rules; Rule 16 and Form 14 of Zambia's Births and Deaths Registration (General Rules); and Zimbabwe's Specimen Certified Copy of an Entry of Birth Registered in the District of Harare.
107 The Botswana Act, sections 6 and 9(1); Malawi Act, section 5; Mauritius Act, section 14; South Africa Act, section 9(1); Tanzania Ordinance, section 11; Swazi Act, section 15(1); Zambian Act, section 14; and Zimbabwe Act, section 11(1).
108 Mauritius Act, section 15.
109 The Botswana Act, sections 6 and 9(1); Malawi Act, section 5; Mauritius Act, section 12(1)(b); South African Act, section 9(1); Tanzania Ordinance, section 11; Swazi Act, section 15(1); Zambian Act, section 14; and Zimbabwe Act, section 11(1).
110 Section 11(2)(b) of the Zimbabwe Act.
111 The Malawi Act, section 7; Swazi Act, section 7; Tanzania Ordinance, section 19; Zambian Registration Rules, Rule 24; and Zimbabwe Act, section 25.
112 The Botswana Act, section 14; South African Act, section 9(3) and Mauritius Act, section12(2).
113 Section 9(3) of the South African Act, and the requirements set out on the Form titled "Application to Register the Birth of a Child who is Over Ten Years" (Form BD 15A) of Tanzania.
114 Sections 6, 12 and 12(1) of the Malawi, Tanzanian and Zimbabwean legislation, respectively.
115 Sections 10(1) and 15 of the Swazi and Zambian Acts, respectively.
116 See the Botswana Act, s 22; the Malawi Act, s 6; Tanzania Ordinance, s 12; the Swazi Act, s 10(2); the South African Act, s 10(b); Zambian Act, s 15 and the Zimbabwe Act, s 12(2).
117 The Malawi Act, s 8; Tanzania Ordinance, s 13; Zambian Act, s 16 and the Zimbabwe Act, s 15.
118 Section 12 of the South African Act.
119 Sections 12(2) and 14 of the Swazi and Zimbabwe Acts, respectively.
120 Section 14(d).
121 Sections 15 and 16 of the Botswana Act; Sections 23-25 of the South African Act; Section 58 of the Mauritius Act; Section 14 of the Tanzania Ordinance; Section 17 of the Zambian Act; and Sections 9, 13 and 18(2) of the Malawi, Swazi and Zimbabwe Acts, respectively.
122 Section 23 of the Botswana Act; Section 11 of the South African and Swazi Acts and section 19 of the Zimbabwe Act.
123 Rule 26 of the Births and Deaths Registration (General) Rules.
124 Malawi Act, s 17; Tanzania Ordinance, s 23 and Zambian Act, s 13.
125 Sections 17 and 18 of the Botswana Act.
126 See the Botswana Act, s 3; Tanzania Ordinance, s 15; Zambian Rules, Rule 42;

Zimbabwe Act, s 3(3) and 4(1) and the Malawi Act, s 10 and the Swazi Act, s 16(2).

127 Malawi Act, s 14; Tanzania Ordinance, s 3(2); Zimbabwe Act, s 5 Botswana Act, s 4(1); Swazi Act, s 6(2)(c) South African Act, s 5; Zambian Act, ss 4 & 8; and Mauritius Act, s 5(1)(iii).

128 Swazi Act, sections 6(1) (deaths) and 22 (external deaths).

129 Mauritius Act, s 38; South African Act, s 14; Swazi Act, s 16(1); Zambian Act, s 5 and the Zimbabwe Act, s 20.

130 The Malawi Act, s 18(2) and (3) and the Tanzania Ordinance, s 26.

131 See section 7 (voluntary registration) and sections 8 and 10 (compulsory registration).

132 See the Botswana Act, s 10; the Malawi Act, s 12; South African Act, s 14; the Swazi Act and Tanzania Ordinance, s 16 and the Zimbabwe Act, s 20(1).

133 Section 38 of the Mauritius Act.

134 South African Act, s 14; Mauritius Act, s 38(b); Botswana Act, s 10; Malawi Act, s 12; Swazi Act, s 16 (death in Swaziland) and 23 (death abroad); the Tanzania Ordinance s 17 and the Zimbabwe Act, s 20(1).

135 Botswana Act, s 14(1) Zimbabwe Act, s. 25(1); Malawi Act, s 12 Tanzania Ordinance, s 17 and Zambian Births and Deaths Registration Rules, Rule 37.

136 Sections 11 and 16 of the Malawi Act and Tanzania Ordinance, respectively.

137 Regulations 7 and 8 of Botswana's Births and Deaths Regulations.

138 Section 20(3) of the Zimbabwe Act.

139 The Zimbabwe Act, section 20(2)-(7) and the Zambian Act, section 18(3)-(7).

140 Sections 14(1) and 15 of the South African Act.

141 Section 44 of the Mauritius Act.

142 See Botswana's Births and Deaths Registration Regulations, Regulation 7 and Form B4; Tanzania's Registration of Births and Deaths Rules, Rule 3 and Form BD.6; Malawi's Births and Deaths Registration (General) Rules, Schedule, Form B; and Zambia's Births and Deaths (General) Rules, Rule 33 & Reg-Gen Form No. 22.

143 Section 39 of the Mauritius Act.

144 Botswana Act, s 13, Malawi Act, s 16, South African Act, s 28(2), Swazi Act, s 28; Zambian Act, s 12 and Zimbabwe Act, s 7.

145 See sections 3(a) and 4(1)(b) of the Namibian Identification Act, 1996 and Swaziland's Identification Order, 1998, respectively.

146 The Preamble to the Act mentions the General Agreement on Trade in Services. See also s 2(1)(n) (one objective of immigration control is to facilitate compliance with the Republic's international obligations). Other sections of the Act make reference to international agreements either as a source of rules for the granting of permits (e.g., treaty permit of s 14) or as a mechanism for the performance of the duties of the Department (e.g., s 2(2)(g)(ii) (one task of the Department is to maintain public records showing funds received or collected from foreign states to defray the cost of repatriating illegal foreigners originating from their country as determined through international relations and agreements)). The DRC migration legislation refers to international conventions in Article 1.

147 Mozambique's Article 2 of Law 5/93 'Exception with regard to special legislation': "The legal regime in respect of foreign citizens shall apply without prejudice to that established in special laws, bilateral or multilateral accords or international conventions of which the Mozambican government is a part."

148 See J Crush and C Tshitereke 'Contesting Migrancy: The Foreign Labor Debate in Post-1994 South Africa' *Africa Today* 48 (2001) 49-70.

149 One might say that the various agreements concluded around issues such as the brain drain and the brain gain constitute another set of relevant international agreements.

150 See generally *www.december18.net.*

151 This convention aims at regulating the conditions under which the migration of persons for employment shall take place and ensuring equality of treatment for migrant workers in certain respects.

152 This convention obliges ratifying States to respect the basic human rights of all migrants for employment and to take steps to determine the existence and suppress clandestine movements of migrants for employment and illegal employment of migrants. The Convention also obliges ratifying States to promote genuine equality of treatment in respect of employment and occupation, social security, trade union and cultural rights, and individual collective freedoms of migrants.

153 Business Day (15 July 2002) (SA DTI official: "Trade in services usually follows trade in goods ... We are talking about financial services, transport services, and telecoms support."). However, the Minister of Home Affairs has suggested that the General Agreement on Trade in Services may stand in the way of preferential access to South Africa for SADC members. See Opening Remarks by Minister Buthelezi at the SAMP/LHR/HSRC Seminar on Regional Integration, Migration, and Poverty, Pretoria, 25 April 2002.

154 Another category of international agreements not discussed here are repatriation agreements and burden-sharing agreements. It does not appear that there are any repatriation agreements presently existing between member states of SADC and OECD countries.

155 F Dava 'A Contribution for the understanding of the legislation on repatriation on Southern Africa: the case of the relations between Mozambique and its neighbours (South Africa, Zimbabwe, and Swaziland)' Seminar on Regional Integration, Migration, and Poverty, Pretoria, 25 April 2002.

156 Report on the South Africa-Lesotho Border (31 May 2001) p. 17.

157 J Oucho and J Crush 'Contra Free Movement: South Africa and the SADC Migration Protocols' *Africa Today* 48 (2001) 139-158.

158 Article 8: SADC Laissez-Passer.

159 See Immigration Act (South Africa) s 2(1)(j)(I)(ee) (one objective of immigration control is to regulate the influx of foreigners and residents in the Republic to promote economic growth by facilitating the movement of students and academic staff within the Southern African Development Community for study, teaching, and research).

160 There is no mention of disease as a grounds of exclusion in the Mozambique statute. However, that statute does not use the prohibited immigrant grounds of the British tradition. Further, the Mozambican law is clear that other regulations may apply (s 16(1)(g)).

161 Mozambique may be the exception here.

162 There are also significant differences in the institutional procedures for applying these exclusion grounds as well as in exempting some persons from the operation of these exclusion grounds.

163 We do not consider asylum or refugee permits which are covered in chapter 5. Furthermore, we do not specifically consider the work rights of a female partner who accompanies a male partner with a temporary employment permit.

164 The South African case of the old and the new laws demonstrates this. In the old legislation, immigration officials would write the purpose onto the visitor's permit. In the new system, the general permit issued will also have a purpose limitation although this is specified in the regulations and is not written in by the immigration official.

165 This Act was not available at the time of writing.

166 There are smaller roles played by other government departments including the Department of Education, the Department of Foreign Affairs and the Department of

Trade and Industry. The Immigration Act (South Africa) also specifically refers to the institutional role and input of other government bodies including the South African Revenue Service, the South African Police Service and the South African National Defence Force. Clause (c) of the Preamble states that the new system of immigration control should ensure that "interdepartmental coordination constantly enriches the functions of immigration control." Section 6 of the Act sets up an interdepartmental liaison committee.

167 This is sometimes enforced through a procedural requirement such as the placement of local adverts.

168 Note that both Mauritius and Swaziland appear to also go one step further than immigration benefits and grant a significant concession for those with financial resources by making citizenship more easily available to such persons. Lesotho's proposal for a new immigration law includes policies to attract investors.

169 These agreements and some information and references concerning them are available at *www.queensu.ca/samp* by clicking on "immigration policy development" and then "bilateral labour agreements."

170 Section 21(4) provides in part that: "In consultation with the Minister of Trade and Industry or Mineral and Energy or Agriculture as the case may be, the Minister of Labour may designate certain industries, or segments thereof, in respect of which the Government may ... (b) enter into agreements with one or more foreign states and set as a condition of a corporate permit that its holder (i) employs foreigners partially, mainly or wholly from such foreign countries; and (ii) remits a portion of the salaries of such foreigners to such foreign countries." Section 231 of the South African Constitution places some conditions on the negotiation of international agreements. These conditions would need to be considered separately for the labour migration and repatriation/readmission aspects of these agreements.

171 In the research for this report, we have not surveyed the constitutional instruments of all countries and other instruments which would allow for a full comparison of the rights of permanent residents and citizens. Note the section of the new Immigration Act 13 of 2002 (South Africa) that nearly equates permanent residence to citizenship and the interpretation section regarding the Citizenship Act's Section 26.

172 In the proposal for a new immigration regime in Lesotho, a formalization of an existing Immigration Board is proposed.

173 The Table of Exclusion and Expulsion Procedures does not address the procedures that implement the non-return obligations of states. These obligations derive from the Refugee Conventions as well as from international human rights treaties such as the Convention Against Torture.

174 We do not know the content of the Mozambican regulations on exclusion.

175 It should be noted that reasons are commonly specifically excluded when the ground of exclusion or expulsion is a Ministerial or Presidential order based on national security.

176 Section 8(5). See also s 30 (declaration of foreigners as undesirable will be as prescribed). The Promotion of Administrative Justice Act 3 of 2000 would on its face require a clear statement of the action taken and notice of the person's rights to appeal and to ask for reasons.

177 A provisional permit was part of the Aliens Control Act 96 of 1991.

178 This paragraph draws in part on work by David Martin.

179 Report on the South Africa-Lesotho Border (31 May 2001) p. 25.

180 In some respects, the Immigration Tribunal, though part of the administrative structures, can be considered as equivalent to a magistrate's court.

181 Zimbabwe also allows for an appeal to a magistrate's court and thus might be con-

sidered to combine the two models, even though the representations to the Minister must be made within 24 hours and there is no obligation on the Minister to respond.

182 South Africa is difficult to classify here until the Immigration Act regulations are made. However, it is perhaps significant that while Section 8 provides for a general package of procedures to govern all immigration decisions, the only significant modifications of the Section 8 package relate precisely to exclusion procedures and to expulsion procedures. This seems to indicate that they will be treated differently.

183 This report has not detailed arrest procedures other than in the chapter on identification and in the section on implementing institutions, where the role of the police has been noted.

184 In Mozambique, it is not clear whether detention pending expulsion is governed by s 29 (administrative expulsion) or by s 41 (clandestine migration).

185 The South African immigration regime makes a distinction between citizens/residents and foreigners in regulating departure.

186 The Table does not cover the regulation of ports of entry. A number of laws do explicitly demarcate the approved ports of entry and exit. The regulation of this matter presumably overlaps significantly with customs regulation.

187 To some extent, this regulation of departure may overlap with the regulation of cross-border movement, regulated in other migration legislation by means of a cross-border pass.

188 This Act also aims to control the movement of Africans to and from Malawi, Zambia, and Zimbabwe.

189 There are also, of course, violations of migration statutes that have legal or civil consequences but no fines or other sanction applicable.

190 Protocol to Prevent, Suppress and Punish Trafficking in Persons, Especially Women and Children, Supplementing the United Nations Convention Against Transnational Organized Crime, G.A. res. 55/25, annex II, 55 U.N. GAOR Supp. (No. 49) at 60, U.N. Doc. A/45/49 (Vol. I) (2001); Protocol Against the Smuggling of Migrants by Land, Sea and Air, Supplementing the United Nations Convention Against Transnational Crime, G.A. res. 55/25, annex III, 55 U.N. GAOR, Supp. (No. 49) at 65, U.N. Doc. A/45/49 (Vol. I) (2001).

191 Report of the UN High Commissioner for Human Rights to the Economic and Social Council: Recommended Principles and Guidelines on Human Rights and Human Trafficking (20 May 2002).

192 http://www.state.gov/g/tip/rls/tiprpt/2002/

193 In a curious symmetry, we did not conduct country interviews in the three countries listed as Tier 2 countries in the USA TIP report. Those countries were the countries of origin for the two researchers (South Africa and Tanzania) as well as Angola.

194 As one official stated: "There is a difference between trafficking and economic migration. The first is consensual and organizers profit. But some young girls from Sudan or Uganda—may be deceived—but feel ashamed to go back—then they would want to apply for asylum. There is a case of two child prostitutes from Bhutan or Thailand that fits in this category. The point is that it is difficult to identify between those trafficked and those who migrated and then are looking for another way to stay."

195 Jonathan Crush and Wade Pendleton, *Regionalizing Xenophobia: Attitudes Towards Immigrants, Migrants and Refugees in Southern Africa* (SAMP Migration Policy Series No. 30, 2003).

196 Dodson argues that it is better to be gender aware than gender blind: "Policy and legislation, therefore, should be written in gender-neutral language only where this is valid, appropriate and intended, and where terms such as "he or she" have a meaningful basis in reality. Where there has been a historical male bias, or where legisla-

tive provisions are likely to have different outcomes for men and women, this should be made explicit rather than left implicit"; see B. Dodson, 'Discrimination by Default? Gender Concerns in South Afican Migration Policy' *Africa Today* 48 (2002) 81.

197 Also, where formal discrimination against women has been removed from legislation, the result is often to adopt a minimal set of standards with respect to protection enjoyed by women. See Dodson 'Discrimination by Default?, 74.

198 To use a conception used by Eve Lester.

199 Additionally, we discuss the place of women in anti-trafficking provisions above.

200 Regulation of the acquisition of citizenship by marriage is discussed specifically in the chapter on citizenship.

201 Some national legislation specifies that persons arrested for migration violations should be treated as prisoners awaiting trial.

202 See *International Migration Policies* 81 (Department of Economic and Social Affairs, Population Division, 1998).

203 See *International Migration Policies* 150-151, 154-155.

204 UNHCR, *Reaching a Balance between Migration Control and Refugee Protection in the European Union: A UNHCR Perspective* (Draft), Geneva, September 2000, paragraph 25.

205 Article 1(A)(2) of the 1951 UN Convention.

206 Article I(1) and (2) of the 1969 OAU Convention.

207 Articles 1(F) and I(5) of the UN and OAU Conventions respectively.

208 Article 14 of the Universal Declaration on Human Rights.

209 Articles 33 and II(3) of the 1951 UN Convention and the 1969 OAU Convention respectively.

210 UNHCR, *op. cit.* paragraphs 41 and 42.

211 Article 31 of the 1951 Convention.

212 The 1951 UN Convention, Preamble and the 1969 OAU Convention, Article II(4).

213 No 9 of 1990, (UNHCR unofficial Translation) Article 1.

214 Of May 1989, Section 2(1).

215 The Refugee Act 1983, Act No. 18 of 1983, Section 3.

216 No 21 of 1991, (UNHCR's unofficial translation) Section 1.

217 No 2 of 1999.

218 No 130 of 1998.

219 No 9 of 1998, Section 4.

220 Refugees Act 1983, Act No. 13 of 1983, Section 3.

221 Cap. 25:01.

222 Section 2 and Schedule.

223 Of 11 April 1978, Section 3.

224 No 40 of 1970, Section 3.

225 Namibian Act, s 4(1)(c) Lesotho Act, s 3(2)(c) and Zambian Act, s 3(1)(d).

226 Section 4(4)(e) .

227 See I van Beek 'Prima Facie Asylum Determination in South Africa: A Description of Policy and Practice' in J Handmaker, L de la Hunt and J Klaaren (eds) *Perspectives on Refugee Protection in South Africa* (Pretoria: Lawyers for Human Rights, 2001), 20-21.

228 G Bruno 'Durable Solutions to the Refugee Problem: UNHCR's Regional Strategy for Southern Africa' in ibid., 70.

229 Angolan Act, Article 4; Lesotho Act, Section 11; Malawi Act, Section 10; Mozambican Act, Article 14, Namibia Act, Section 26 and South African Act, Section 2.

230 For extended commentary on this provision see B Rutinwa *Refugee Admission and Asylum Procedures in Tanzania* (Dar-es-Salaam: Centre for the Study of Forced Migration, University of Dar es Salaam, 2001), 17.

231 See Articles 7 and 9 of the Mozambican Act and Section 21 of the South African Act and Section 2(2) of the Refugee Regulations of April 2000.

232 Lesotho Act, Section 9 and the Zimbabwe Act, Sections 8 and 9.

233 Angolan Act, Article 18; Botswana Act, Section 13; Namibian Act, Section 16(b); the South African Act, Section 27(c) and Zimbabwe Act, Section 10(b).

234 Section 10 of the Swazi Order and Section 10 of the Zambian Act.

235 Rutinwa *Refugee Admission and Asylum Procedures* 20.

236 Lesotho Act, s 3(1)(c); South African Act, s 35(1); Tanzanian Act, s 4(1)(c); Zambian Act, s 3(1); Swazi Order, s 3(1) and Zimbabwe Act, s 3(2).

237 Angolan Act, s 16; Malawi Act, s 6(1)(a).

238 Namibian Act, s 13 and Zimbabwe Act, s 7(4)(a).

239 Botswana Act, ss 5 and 8; Mozambican Act, ss 8 and 3; Lesotho Act, s 7; Tanzanian Act, s 9; and Zambia (interview).

240 Botswana Act, s 8(2); Tanzanian Act, ss 9(7) and (8); Zimbabwea Act, s 7(6) and Zambia (interview).

241 Sections 27 and 28 of the Zimbabwe Act.

242 Lesotho Act, s 7(10)

243 Article 3(2).

244 Angolan Act, Article 19; Mozambican Act, Article 2((3); South African Act, ss 27(d) and (e); Swazi Order, s 6(2); Zambian Act, s (2) and Zimbabwe Act, s 10(1).

245 Tanzanian Act, Section 16; Zambian Act, Section 12; Namibian Act, Section 20 and Swazi Order, Section 12.

246 South African Act, Section 22(b).

247 Section 35(2).

248 Botswana Act, Section 9, provisos (i) and (ii).

249 Angolan Act, Articles 18 and 21; Lesotho Act, Section 13 and Mozambican Act, Articles 5(1) and (2).

250 Angolan Act, Article 8 and South African Act, Section 27(f).

251 See Malawi Government, Statement Presented at the First Meeting of the Commonwealth Intergovernmental Group on Refugees and Displaced Persons, London, 3 October 1996, Appendix 1b.

252 See Malawi Government, Statement Presented at the First Meeting of the Commonwealth Intergovernmental Group on Refugees and Displaced Persons, London, 3 October 1996, Appendix 1b.

253 See a document titled "Civil Status Division" on the website of the Ministry of Defence and Home Affairs: http://ncb.intnet.mu/dha/ministry/civil.htm

254 It is suggested that MIDSA not take the EU (or indeed any other regional grouping as a model) but instead be cognisant of the Berne initiative which takes a global and minimalist approach to best practices of migration management.

255 See Guideline 4 of the UN High Commissioner for Human Rights: 'Ensuring an adequate legal framework': "The lack of specific and/or adequate legislation on trafficking at the national level has been identified as one of the major obstacles in the fight against trafficking. There is an urgent need to harmonize legal definitions, procedures, and cooperation at the national and regional levels in accordance with international standards. The development of an appropriate legal framework that is consistent with relevant international instruments and standards will also play an important role in the prevention of trafficking and related exploitation."

256 The legal focus of this suggestion undoubtedly comes in part from the legal professional training of the authors of this report. But additionally, legal provisions represent the most formal aspects of the migration regime. As such they are likely to per-

sist and not succumb to the factors of time, distance, language barriers and relative lack of resources that characterize the SADC region. If attended to, legal provisions may serve as vehicles for non-legal as well as legal avenues of harmonization.

257 T Maluwa, 'The Refugee Problem in Post-Apartheid Southern Africa' in T Maluwa *International Law in Post Colonial Africa* (The Hague: Kluwer International Law, 1999) 195.

Table 1: Citizenship Source of Authority

SADC Country	Primary Source of Citizenship Rules	Collected Citizenship Documents
Angola	Law 13 of 1991 (13 May 1991)	
Botswana	Citizenship Act 8 of 1998	Citizenship Act 8 of 1998 Citizenship Act 25 of 1982 as amended by S.I. 148 of 1982 and Act 17 of 1984 Citizenship Regulations (4 February 1983) Deprivation of Citizenship (No. 1) Order, 1989
Lesotho	Lesotho Citizenship Order 16 of 1971 Last Amended in 1989	Lesotho Citizenship Order 16 of 1971 with some amendment annotations
Malawi	Malawi Citizenship Act of 1966 Amended in 1967 Amended in 1971	Malawi Citizenship Act of 1966 as amended Malawi Citizenship (Prescribed Languages) Regulations Malawi Citizenship (Forms and Fees) Regulations
Mauritius	Chapter III, Constitution of Mauritius Last amended by Act 23 of 1995 Mauritius Citizenship Act (14 December 1968) Last amended by Act 24 of 1995	Chapter III, Constitution of Mauritius as amended Mauritius Citizenship Act as amended
Mozambique	Nationality Act of June 1975 Last amended by Act 16 of 1987 (This statute is considered to be a part of the Constitution)	Nationality Act of June 1975 as amended (unofficial translation) Reacquisition of Nationality Act 2 of 1982 (unofficial translation)
Namibia	Article 4, Constitution of Namibia	Article 4, Constitution of Namibia

	Namibian Citizenship Act 14 of 1990	Namibian Citizenship Act 14 of 1990 Namibian Citizenship Special Conferment Act 14 of 1991
Seychelles	Citizenship of Seychelles Act (29 June 1976) 1993 Constitution, chapter II, citizenship articles 7-14	
South Africa	South African Citizenship Act 88 of 1995 Amended by Act 69 of 1997	South African Citizenship Act 88 of 1995 as amended
Swaziland	Swaziland Citizenship Act 14 of 1992	Swaziland Citizenship Act 14 of 1992
Tanzania	Tanzania Citizenship Act 6 of 1995	Tanzania Citizenship Act 6 of 1995 (incomplete copy) Tanzania Citizenship Regulations, 1997
Zambia	Part II "Citizenship" of the Constitution of Zambia, 1991 as amended by Act 18 of 1996 Citizenship of Zambia Act 26 of 1975 Last amended by Act 10 of 1990	Part II "Citizenship" of the Constitution of Zambia, 1991 as amended by Act 18 of 1996 Citizenship of Zambia Act 26 of 1975 Citizenship of Zambia (Amendment) Act 24 of 1988 Citizenship of Zambia (Amendment) Act 10 of 1990
Zimbabwe	Chapter II, Constitution of Zimbabwe Last amended by Act 9 of 1993 Citizenship of Zimbabwe Act 23 of 1984 Amended by Act 7 of 1990 Last amended in 2001	Chapter II, Constitution of Zimbabwe as amended Citizenship of Zimbabwe Act 23 of 1984 as amended in 1990 Newspaper report of S.I. 217 of 2001 Citizenship of Zimbabwe (Renunciation of Foreign Citizenship) Regulations

Table 2: *Soli* and *Sanguinis*

SADC Country	Jus Soli Territorial Right to Citizenship	Jus Sanguinis (First Generation) Right to Citizenship of Children of Citizen Parent	Jus Sanguinis (Second Generation) Right to Citizenship of Children of Parent Whose Citizenship Derives From Descent
Angola	No (exception only for statelessness)	Yes	Yes
Botswana	No	Yes	Yes
Democratic Republic of Congo	No	Yes	Yes
Lesotho	Yes (but subject to registration and choice of nationality at 21)	Yes, if born outside Lesotho	
Malawi	No (exception for unknown parents)	Yes, if born in Malawi and parent is of African race or if born outside Malawi and parent is of African race and is native-born	No, unless born in Malawi and parent is of African race
Mauritius	No (yes for persons born before 1 September 1995)	Yes	No, unless born in Mauritius
Mozambique	Yes (citizenship or second foreign general and citizenship for first foreign generation unless contrary declaration by parents at birth and no declaration by individual at age 18)	Yes, if born in Mozambique or if born outside Mozambique and registration and choice of nationality at age 18	Yes
Namibia	Yes, if one parent is ordinarily resident or if child would otherwise be stateless	Yes, if born outside Namibia and upon registration	Yes

Seychelles	No (exception for unknown parents or statelessness)	Yes, if born in wedlock and in Seychelles or if born to an out of wedlock citizen mother with an unknown father	Yes, but if born abroad must register
South Africa	Yes, if one parent is citizen or permanent resident	Yes, if born outside South Africa and registered	Yes
Swaziland	No	Yes, if father is a Swazi citizen	Yes, but if born abroad must register
Tanzania	No	Yes, if born in Tanzania or if born outside Tanzania and father is citizen	Yes
Zambia	Yes, but only for children of established residents and must apply to Citizenship Board for confirmation at age 21	Yes	Yes
Zimbabwe			

1. June 27, 2002: In the making of this table, we are not putting in the additional information regarding the election provisions many SADC countries have in order to tolerate dual nationals up until age 18 or 21. See Angola (18), Botswana (21), DRC (21), Lesotho (21), Malawi (21), Mozambique (18), Namibia (18), Tanzania (21), Zambia (22). The dual nationality policies of other countries are either more or less complex: Mauritius, Seychelles, South Africa, Swaziland, and Zimbabwe. This information seems very relevant to the second-generation *jus sanguinis* column in Southern Africa.
2. This table is based on the rules for currently born persons. A number of countries have different rules for persons born before specific dates: Botswana (31 December 1982), Lesotho (3 October 1966), Malawi (6 July 1966), Namibia (21 March 1990), Seychelles (29 June 1976), Tanzania (9 December 1961). These regime changes (appear to) relate to independence.

Table 3: Citizenship by Naturalization

SADC Country	Renunciation Requirement at Naturalization	Residence Requirement	Knowledge of Language	Other
Botswana	No	10 of 12 years, including 12 months immediately preceding application and must have lodged declaration of intention 5 to 6 years earlier	Setswana or any other tribal community language	Notice procedure, oath, good character
Lesotho	Yes	5 years	Sesotho or English	Oath, good character/police clearance, financially solvent
Malawi	Yes	7 years	Prescribed vernacular or English	Oath, good character, financially solvent, suitable citizen, sponsor's certificates
Mauritius	Yes	12 months plus 5 of 7 years preceding that 12 months	English or any other language current in Mauritius	Oath, good character knowledge of responsibilities
Mozambique	Not per se but must give "assurances of political and moral integration in society"	5 years	None	No sentence for crime against security of the people
Namibia	Yes	5 years	None	Oath, good character, knowledge of responsibilities, police clearance

Seychelles	No Constitution makes provision for dual nationality	Ordinarily resident in the Republic for a period of 5 yrs immediately preceding that date	Adequate knowledge of English of French or any language which may be prescribed	Good charac-ter, intention to continue to reside in Seychelles, enter or con-tinue in the service of the Government, has knowledge of the respon-sibilities of a citizen of Seychelles, has not been refused natu-ralization as a citizen within the period of 2 years immedi-ately preceding his application.
South Africa	No	Permanent residence and 12 months immediately prior and a further 4 of 8 years preceding application; possibility of exception	One of eleven official languages	Oath, good character, knowledge of responsibilies
Swaziland "registration"	Not explicitly but ministerial discretion	12 months immediately prior and 5 of 7 years before application	Siswati or English	Oath, good character, adequate means of support
Tanzania	Yes, subject to legal possibility	12 months immediately prior plus residence in 7 of 10 years before	Swahili or English	Good character, financially solvent, sponsors' certificates, notice procedure

Zambia "registration"	Yes	10 years	English or any prescribed indigenous language	Oath, good character
Zimbabwe "registration"	Yes	5 years, with exceptions	none	Oath, good character, intention to continue to reside, rejected applications and applications from former citizens are not to be consiered for two years.

Table 4: Citizenship by Marriage

SADC Country	Separate Provision for Naturalization by Marriage?	Comparison with Naturalization Requirements
Botswana	Yes (s 14)	Two a half year notice period; aggre gate residence of five years; both with exceptions.
Lesotho	Yes (s 7)	No period of residence required.
Malawi	Yes (s 16)	Five years residence. [Limited to wives].
Mauritius	Yes (Con s 24 and s 7)	4 years of living "with his spouse under the same conjugal roof in Mauritius".
Mozambique	Yes (article 10)	No period of residence, no age requirement.
Namibia	Yes (Con article 4(3))	Subsequent residence in Namibia as spouse for two years.
South Africa	Yes (s 5(5))	Permanent residence and two years married residence in South Africa
Swaziland	Yes (s 8)	Upon declaration and proof of marriage; not available to spouses of citizens by registration. [Limited to women].
Tanzania	Yes (s 11)	Upon application during life of husband (provided woman has not previously renounced or been deprived of citizenship). [Limited to women.]
Zambia	No	
Zimbabwe	Yes (Con s 7(2))	Upon registration during subsistence of marriage. [Limited to women.]

Table 5: Citizenship by Registration

SADC Country	Pre-Independence Claimants	Preferred Countries of Origin	Adoption/ Minor	Other
Botswana	30 September 1966 Settlement (s 6)		Adoption (ss 7, 8), Minors (s 9)	Presidential (s 10)
Lesotho	4 October 1966: (ss 3, 4)	Commonwealth and prescribed countries (s 9)	Minors (s 11)	
Malawi	5 July 1966: (s 3)	Commonwealth (s 13), African States (s 14)	Minors (s 17)	Close connection with Malawi (s 15), Minister and special circumstances (s 19)
Mauritius	12 March 1968: (Con ss 20, 21)	Commonwealth (s 5)	Adoption (s 3), Minors (s 6)	Incorporation of territory (s 4)
Mozambique	Date of Independence 1975: (ss 1, 3, 4, 5, 6, 9)		Minors (s 13)	
Namibia	21 March 1990: (Con s 4(4); see also Act 14 of 1991)		Minors (s 5(4))	Honorary citizenship (s 6)
Seychelles			Adoption s (3)(1) Minors s (4)(1)	Presidential s (5)
South Africa	See Act 196 of 1993		Minors (s 5(4)) ("naturalization")	
Swaziland	See Act 36 of 1967 and Order 22 of 1974			
Tanzania	26 April 1964: (s 4)		Minors (s 10) ("naturalization")	
Zambia			Adoption (s 11), Minors (s 12)	Presidential (s 13)
Zimbabwe	Appointed day: (Con s 7(1))		Adoption (Con s 7(4), Minors (Con s 7(3))	Honorary citizenship (s 17)

Table 6: Dual Citizenship

SADC Country	Provisions on Dual Citizenship?	Tolerance?	Policy Basis	Other Policy
Botswana	Yes (s 15)	Yes		Loss of citizenship unless renunciation by age of majority.
Democratic Republic of Congo	Yes (Con s 9)	No	Prohibition on dual citizenship.	
Lesotho	Yes (ss 8, 19)	Yes		Loss of citizenship unless renunciation at age of majority (within five years?); duty of renunciation for citizens by naturalization and registration; liability to deprivation for exercise of rights of citizenship
Malawi	Yes (ss 6, 7, 8, 9, 10)	No	Dual citizens with knowledge liable to deprivation; loss of citizenship unless renunciation by age of majority; loss of citizenship upon acquisition (one year election period for marriage and involuntary acquisition)	

Mauritius	Yes (ss 12, 14)	Yes		Liability to deprivation for citizens by registration and naturalization if exercise of other citizenship rights; Minister may withhold registration of renunciation.
Mozambique	Yes (s 14)	No	Loss of citizenship upon acquisition.	
Namibia	Yes (ss 7, 26)	No	Loss of citizenship upon acquisition; prohibition on dual citizenship.	
Seychelles	Yes Art 13 (2) of the Constitution of Seychelles 1993	Yes	Person shall make a declaration to the citizenship officer	
South Africa	Yes (ss 6(1)(a), 8(2), 9)	Yes		Liability to deprivation upon voluntary acquisition other than marriage; liability to deprivation upon conviction; liability to deprivation upon exercise of citizenship rights.
Swaziland	None	De facto		
Tanzania	Yes (s 14)	Yes		Liability to deprivation upon exercise of citizenship rights
Zambia	Yes (Con s 9, s 19)	Yes		Loss of citizenship upon voluntary

					acquisition (not including marriage) or exercise of citizenship at full age; loss of citizenship for naturalized citizens upon involuntary acquisition.
Zimbabwe	Yes (s 9)	No	Prohibition on full age dual citizenship.	

Table 7: Loss of Citizenship

SADC Country	Fraud	Criminal Conviction	Voluntary Acquisition or Exercise of Foreign Citizenship	National Security or Disloyalty	Extended Foreign Residence	Comments
Botswana	yes	No	Yes (all citizens)	yes	Yes, 7 years	Limited to citizens by registration or natural-ization
Lesotho	yes	Yes, 5 years	yes	yes	Yes, 7 years	Limited to citizens by registration or natural-ization
Malawi	yes	Yes, 12 months (within 7 years)	yes	yes	Yes, 7 years	Not applica-ble to citizens by birth or descent
Mauritius	yes	Yes, 12 months (within	yes	yes	Yes, 5 years	Limited to citizens by registration

		7 years)				or natural-ization
Mozambique				Yes (includes any office in a foreign state)	yes	
Namibia	yes	Yes, 12 months	yes	yes	Yes, permanent residence and 2 years	Limited to citizens by registration or naturalization
South Africa	Yes (only for naturalization)	Yes (only for dual citizens), 12 months	yes	Yes (only for dual citizens)	no	
Swaziland	yes	no	yes	no	Yes, 7 years	Limited to citizens by registration or naturalization
Tanzania	Yes	Yes, 12 months (within 5 years)	Yes (not citizens by birth)	yes	Yes, 5 years	Limited to citizens by naturalization
Zambia	yes	No (only for trafficking)	yes	yes	Yes, 7 years	Limited to citizens by registration
Zimbabwe	yes	Yes, 12 months (within 5 years)	yes	yes	Yes, 7 years	Limited to citizens by registration

Table 8: Reacquisition Policies

SADC Country	Eligible Class of Former Citizen	Revocable Grounds of Loss	Conditions of Reacquisition	Other
Botswana	Birth, Descent	Dual citizenship, renunciation	Residency, renunciation, and intention to reside	
Lesotho	Any	Dual citizenship, renunciation	Renunciation, oath	
Malawi	Any	Any	Renunciation, oath	
Mauritius	Any	Dual citizenship, renunciation	renunciation	Special provisional renunciation for married persons
Mozambique	Any	Any	Residency, political and moral assurances of reintegration	Special provision for reacquisition by married women
Namibia	Any	Dual citizenship, renunciation, deprivation by criminal conviction	Renunciation	
Seychelles				
South Africa	Any	Any	Permanent residence for former citizens by registration and naturalization, residence for former citizens by birth and descent	
Swaziland				No explicit provision
Zambia	Any	Any	Application to Citizenship Board, evidence	

			of lack of knowledge of loss of citizenship	
Zimbabwe	Any	Any except voluntary renunciation	Renunciation (exception if consent of President), oath	

Table 9: Grounds for Exclusion

SADC Country	Economic	Disease	Past Criminal Convictions or Activity	National Security	Prior Violations of Migration Laws	Prostitution or Living on Proceeds	Other Exclusion Grounds (not including dependants
Botswana (s 7)	yes	yes	yes	Yes (s 27 (1))	no	yes	Presidential declaration
Lesotho (First Schedule)	yes	yes	yes	yes	yes	no	
Malawi (s 5)	yes	yes	yes	yes	Prior deportation	Yes or if homosexual	Deeming on standard or habits of life, Illiteracy
Mauritius (s 8)	yes	yes	yes	yes	no	yes	Habitual beggars or vagrants, Chronic alcoholics, drug addic-

							tion, traffic in drugs
Mozam-bique (s 16)	yes			Yes (s 29)	yes		
Namibia (s 39)	yes	yes	Yes	yes	yes	no	Deeming on account of stan-dard or habits of life
South Africa (ss 29, 30)	yes	yes	Yes, as well as warrant issued, includes genocide and torture	Ministerial identifi-cation as undesir-able	Prior deporta-tion or order to depart	no	Member of orga-nization advoca-ting of hatred or using crime or terror-ism;
Swaziland (s 3)	yes	yes	Yes	yes	Yes, prohibi-ted or ordered to leave	no	Failure to prod-uce a passport; deemed class of persons, entry or presence unlawful in terms of other law
Tanzania (s 10)	yes	yes	Yes	Ministerial deeming	yes	yes	Ministerial deeming, dealing in danger-ous drugs
Zambia (s 22 and Second Schedule)	Yes (if no valid permit)	yes	Yes if foreign conviction and if	Ministerial declara-tion	Yes, prohibi-ted or ordered	yes	Presence in Zambia for three months

			not of good character		to leave, revoked or expired permit, illegal entrants		of 12 months without permit
Zimbabwe (s 14)	yes	yes	Yes	Ministerial deeming	Yes, prohibited or prior deportation or ordered to leave	Yes or if homosexual	Deemed on standards or habits of life

Table 10: Types of Temporary Permit

SADC Country	Visitor/ General	Study	Treaty	Medical	Relative	Work	Investors	Corporate	Retired	Exchange	Cross-border	Other
Botswana	Y, 90 days				N							
DRC	Y, 6 months										Exemption	
Lesotho	Temporary Permit (s 7)											
Malawi	Y, 90 days	Y				Y	Y					Temporary permit to prohibited immigrant
Mauritius	Y, 6 months				Y	N						
Mozam-bique	Y, 90 days	Y				N						
Namibia	Y, 12 months	Y			Y	Y						
Seychelles	Y, 3 months				Y	Y						To prohibited

												immigrant
South Africa	Y, 90 days /3 years	Y	Y	Y	Y	Y	Y	Y	Y	Y	Y	
Swaziland	Y, 6 months	Y			Y	Y	Y					Prohibited Immigrant Pass, Special Pass
Tanzania	Y, 90 days		Y		Y	Y	Y					Special Pass, Re-Entry Pass, Landing Pass
Zambia	Y, 90 days	Y			Y	Y	Y					Temporary Permit to Prohibited Immigrant
Zimbabwe	Y, 6 months	Y		Y	Y	Y						Temporary Permit

Table 11: Permits and Visa Authorities

SADC Country	Temporary Permit Authority	Employment Permit Authority	Investors Permit Authority	Visa Authority
Botswana	general visitors with 90 day limit (s 17)	Employment of Non-Citizens Act 11 of 1981	Same; reg 2(b): work permit for self-employed persons	Immigration (Visa) Regulations; visa required to make travel document valid, except for listed countries; .
DRC	Ordonnance No 87 -281 du 13 Aout 1987	La legislation du travail	Article 7 of Ordonnance No 87-281 du 13 Aout 1987	Article 2 of Ordonnance No 87-281 du 13 Aout 1987
Lesotho	temporary permit (s 7); distinguished	Department of Labour legi-		

	visitors (s 9)	slation and s 7 and First Schedule	
Malawi	Temporary residence permit (s 26); visitor's permits, 90 day limit (s 28); student's permit (s 33); temporary permit to prohibited immigrant (s 18)	Temporary employment permits (s 27)	Business residence permits (s 24A); policy statement on employment of expatriates and employment permit guide	
Mauritius	Residence permits (s 9)	Non-Citizens Employment Restriction Act	See s 9(3) of Citizenship Act	Passport Act (14 February 1969) (s 12)
Mozambique	Tourist visa (90 days) (s 11); visitor's visa (90 days) (s 13); business visa (90 days) (s 14); student visa (12 months) (s 15)	Laws 25 and 26 of 1999 (24 May 1999)		Passport with visa gives authorization to reside (s 17)
Namibia	Students permits (s 28); visitors permits with 12 month limit (s 29)	Employment permits (s 27)		Requirement of passport with visa (s 12)
Seychelles	Visitors (s16) Prohibited immigrants (s18)	Gainful occupation (s17)		Immigration Decree
South Africa	Visitors permit (90 days/3 years) (s 11); diplomatic permit (s 12); study permit (s 13); treaty permit (s 14); crew permit (s 16); medical treatment permit (s 17); relative's permit (s 18); retired person's permit (s 20); exchange permit (s 22); cross-border and transit pass (s 24)	Work permits (s 19)	Business permit (s 15); corporate permit (s 21)	As prescribed; required for a visitor's permit (s 11(1)(a)) unless for citizens of certain prescribed countries with certain prescribed financial guarantees in respect of departure
Swaziland	Immigration	Schedule (s 5):	Person with	Immigration

	Regulations (s 18): dependant's pass (reg 15), student's pass (reg 17), visitor's pass (reg 19) (6 months limit), transit pass (reg 21), prohibited immigrant's pass (reg 23), and a special pass (reg 24).	Specific Employment by Specific Employer (Class A, B); missionary (Class C), agriculture (Class D), mining (Class E), trade, business, or profession (Class F), manufacture (Class G); Prescribed Professions (Class H)	sufficient income or investment capital (Class I)	Regulations (s 18): reg 34 and Sixth Schedule read with s 10 of the Passports Act (requiring visas as regulated)
Tanzania	Immigration Regulations: dependant's pass (reg 9); in-transit pass (reg 11); special pass (reg 12); visitor's pass (reg 13) with 90 day limit; re-entry pass (reg 14); inter-state pass (reg 15); Landing pass (reg 16)	Trade, business, profession, agriculture, mining, or manufacture (Class A, s 19); specified employment (Class B, s 20); Other (Class C).	Large Capital Investors, Class A	None; s 15 mandates entry with passport and a permit or pass
Zambia	Visitor's permit (s 15) within 90 days; study permits (s 16); temporary permit to prohibited immigrant (s 17); relatives of permit holders (s 14 and Class C of First Schedule); relatives of citizen (s 14 and Class D of First Schedule)	Employment permit (s 18 and Class A of First Schedule)	Financial resources (s 14 and Class B of First Schedule); see Rules Governing the Issuance of Employment Permits to Expatriate Personnel and Self-Employment Permits to Investors	Definition of passport (s 2) includes a visa; see Guidelines on the Issuance, Extension of Permits, Visa Requirements and Procedures

| Zimbabwe | Visitor's entry certificate (s 31 and reg 42) within 6 month limit; Immigration regulations (s 19): temporary permit (reg 25); student permit (s 31); scholars permit (s 34); dependant's ("alien's") permit (reg 37); permit relating to prescribed diseases (reg 39) | Immigration Regulations (s 19): temporary employment permit (reg 22) | | None: see visitor's entry certificate and permits |

Table 12: Employment and Investment Policies

SADC Country	Employment Permit Factors	Investment Permits
Botswana	Effect on domestic employment; Employer training arrangements;	Same (reg 2(b))
DRC		5 years non-renewable, new business establishment
Lesotho	Effect on social and economic interests of residents in area where alien is to sojourn; Specific employment sectors approved by Minister	
Malawi	Limitation to geographical area; limitation to specific occupation; limitation to specific employer;	Payment of prescribed fee; Policy on Employment of Expatriates: Limitation of five

	Policy on Employment Permit Guide (for time posts): factors are qualifications as compared with advert, experience, relative importance of post in organization, availability of local expertise, period of stay of expatriate if renewed, local advert process, and remuneration package.	key posts, two key posts for USD 100,000; one factor is shortage of domestic qualified workers;
Mauritius	Specific employer limitation; External application; Limit of three years for skilled workers;	5000 USD investment and two years residence for citizenship (s 9(3) of Citizenship Act); Perm Res upon USD 500,000 investment in qualified business through bank
Mozambique	Laws 25/99 and Laws 26/99	same
Namibia	Sufficient qualifications; Insufficient number of domestic workers; Application to Immigrant Selection Board	
Seychelles		
South Africa	Quota work permit (s 19(1)): category as prescribed, quota available; General work permit (s 19(2)): diligent search for domestic workers, prevailing wage, notification on change of position; Intra-company transfer	Business permit (s 15): prescribed financial or capital contribution, certified compliance Corporate permit (s 21): prevailing wage, financial deportation guarantees, representations on percentage of citizens and other prescribed matters.

	work permit (s 19(5)): financial guarantees of deportation costs, certified need for foreigner, specific employer limitation	
Swaziland	Specific employer limitation with exceptions for sectors including trade, business, and professions; Specification of steps to engage domestic workers; Requirement for effective training programmes	Class I: foreign income of prescribed amount
Tanzania	Specific employer limitation (s 20): USD 500 Specific sectors including trade, business, and professions (s 19): USD 1500 (large capital investors), USD 500 (small cap), or USD 50 (peasants)	Large capital investors: USD 1500 fee
Zambia	Professional qualification or financial resources; Insufficient number of domestic workers; Benefit to inhabitants generally	Sufficient financial resources to maintain self; Presence a benefit to inhabitants generally
Zimbabwe	Specific employer and employment limitation;	Possesses substantial financial means and is prepared to invest substantially in Zimbabwe without engaging in any occupation (reg 16(1)l)

◇ Table 13: Permanent Residence Policies

SADC Country	Factors Considered in Decision	Procedures	Other Procedures
Botswana (ss 18-23)	Sufficient qualifications, education, experience etc. to render applicant efficient or, if not, in a position to support himself;	Immigrant Selection Boards, Regional Boards;	Ministerial power to issue PR permit to desirable person; Ministerial exemption to a class of persons; Ministerial discretion to grant PR after ten years of lawful presence.
DRC (art 8)	Sufficient personal means; compatibility with security and public morality		
Lesotho (s 6)	Effect on social and economic interests of residents in area where alien is to sojourn; Specific employment sectors approved by Minister	External application; Minister	
Malawi (s 24)	Desirable immigrant	Minister; internal application;	Ministerial exemption (s 25)
Mauritius	Specific employer limitation; External application; Limit of three years for skilled workers; Issued to fit work permit in terms of Employment (Non-Citizens) Restriction Act		
Mozambique (ss 21(2))	10 years of temporary status yields PR	automatic	
Namibia (s 26)	Good character; Sufficient means or skills; Will assimilate within a reasonable time after entry and be a desirable inhabitant; Insufficient number of domestic workers;	Immigrant Selection Board	

Seychelles	Not a prohibited immigrant Intends to remain in Seychelles for a period in excess of 3 months Has family or domestic connection Has made or will make in the opinion of the Minister some special contribution to the economic, social or cultural life of Seychelles	Minister	
South Africa	Five years of work permit plus offer of permanent employment at prevailing wage; Spouse of citizen or PR with good faith spousal relationship; Offer of permanent employment, dvertised and no qualified domestic workers, prevailing wage, and within quotas; Business PR (s 27I) with prescribed net worth of establishment: Investor's PR)s 27(f) for prescribed fee; relative's PR, first step of kinship to citizen/ resident (s 27(g)	Automatic; Automatic; Application to Department; Same; Same; Same;	
Swaziland	None, see citizenship		
Tanzania	Not explicitly, see temporary employment permits		
Zambia	Professional qualification or financial resources; Insufficient number of domestic workers; Benefit to inhabitants generally (same as temporary employment permits) (s 18)		

Zimbabwe	Spouse or relative of citizen or PR; Substantial financial means; Temporary employment permit for five years (reg 16) (waiver of two of the five years for USD 300,000)	Application to Chief Immigration Officer	

Table 14: Exclusion and Expulsion Procedures

SADC Country	Procedures at Exclusion	Link of Exclusion Grounds to Expulsion Grounds (apart from non–return)?	Expulsion Legislation	Expulsion Procedures
Botswana (s 11)	Notice and grounds for determination as prohibited immigrant, appeal within 3 days to magistrate's court	Yes, prohibited immigrant status	(s 13)	same
Lesotho (ss 39, 40)	Procedures for Commonwealth and reciprocating countries citizens; else no notice or appeal	No, refusal of leave to enter only one form of unlawfulness leading to expulsion (s 14)	(s 25)	same
Malawi (ss 9, 10)	Notification and opportunity for representations for public charge and insufficient means exclusion, no appeal; generally, notice and appeal to magistrate's	Yes, prohibited immigrant status	(ss 8, 11)	same

	court within 3 days.			
Mauritius (s 8)	If claim to residence or citizenship, appeal to Minister, possibility of a provisional permit, appeal to Supreme Court; else no appeal.	No, prohibited immigrant status only one of four grounds of expulsion	Deportation Act (14 December 1968) (s 5)	Notification and sufficient particulars; warrant issued by Magistrate; report by Magistrate; order by Minister (not bound by Magistrate).
Mozambique (s 5(2))	Subject to regulation	No, expulsion grounds only some of exclusion grounds	(ss 29-37)	8 day investigation, expulsion, internal or court appeal (s 29)
Namibia (ss 10, 11)	Notification in writing, no appeal; possibility of a 2 month provisional permit, investigation and notification in writing.	Yes, prohibited immigrant status	(ss 42, 43, 44)	Arrest without warrant, such investigations as deemed necessary, decision, notification in writing, opportunity for self-expulsion, else application to Immigration Tribunal for authorization of expulsion with 3 days notice, hearing with legal representation permitted, warrant for removal
Seychelles				
South Africa (ss 8, 30(2))	Application for waiver of grounds of undesirability; notification in writing of rights and "other prescribed matters";	Yes, prohibited person status and undesirable person status	(ss 8, 34)	Arrest without warrant, notification of deportation and right to appeal and right to request a warrant;

	appeal to DG (10 days) and Minister (20 days) with no obligation to respond; once final, appeal to Magistrate's Court.			appeal to DG (10 days); appeal to Minister (20 days) with no obligation to respond; once final, appeal to a Magistrate's court.
Swaziland (reg 25, s 5(3))	Written notice of exclusion; appeal to Minister; possibility of prohibited immigrant's pass for 3 months; no appeal to Court.	No, prohibited immigrant status only one source of unlawfulness leading to expulsion	(s 8, reg 25)	Minister shall seek advice of Immigration Advisory Committee before making expulsion order; but immigrant officer may make expulsion order to prohibited immigrant with notification.
Tanzania (s 12, reg 17)	Notification in writing, taken before a magistrate on demand, unless declared prohibited	No, prohibited immigrant status only one of grounds for expulsion	(s 14, reg 16/17)	Ministerial order in writing; else notification in writing
Zambia (ss 17, 23, 24)	Notification in writing of requirement to leave within 48 hours; possibility of a temporary permit for 30 days; written representations to the Minister after 7 days of lawful presence;	No, prohibited immigrant status only one of grounds for expulsion	(s 26)	Without warrants for prohibited immigrants or those suspected to be prohibited immigrants; warrants for those under Ministerial order.
Zimbabwe (ss 8(4), 18, 21, 23, reg 45)	Notification of refusal of leave to enter specifying the provision of the act used; no right to	Yes, prohibited immigrant status	(ss 8(2), 8(3), 21, 23)	Notification in writing to prohibited immigrants; representations to

make representations or appeal if suspected prohibited immigrant on economic grounds, past criminal conviction, or Ministerial deeming; if declared or suspected on other grounds, right to make representations within 24 hours, no obligation to respond, provisional pass on some grounds; appeal to Magistrate's Court within 3 days			Minister within 24 hours, no obligation to respond; appeal to Magistrate's Court within 3 days

Table 15: Detention Policies

SADC Country	Detention at the Border	Detention Pending Expulsion
Botswana	s 10: 14 day limit, reported to Minister, Ministerial extensions beyond 14 days, prison/gaol; bond possible	S 14: any period as necessary, prison.
Lesotho	S 34(2): immigration office, prison, gaol or other prescribed place.	Same
Malawi	S 15: 14 day limit, prison/gaol, bond possible	S 16: prison or other authorized place of custody
Mauritius	Ss 13, 20: if appealing refusal to admit, detained pending decision by Minister	S 28 (Deportation Act): detention may be ordered by magistrate pending decision by Minister, 28 day limit
Mozambique	S 41: Clandestine migration is punishable in terms of law in force	

Namibia	S 42: detention pending investigations, 14 day limit, Ministerial extension, bond possible,	Detention pending application for authorization to remove (s 42), may be detained after refusal to leave (s 50/51)
South Africa	same	S 34: place under control or administration of the Department, can request confirmation by warrant of Court, limit of 30 days without warrant, minimum prescribed standards of detention protecting his or her dignity and relevant human rights, forced payment of costs possible
Swaziland	S 13(2): police custody, as long as necessary	S 8(3)(b): custody "until his departure"
Tanzania	S 12: person arrested may be conducted to and placed across frontier; if declared prohibited immigrant, may be placed in custody	S 14: custody awaiting deportation, no limit for Ministerial order, 28 days for court order
Zambia	Ss 25, 36: 14 day limit, any place specially provided, a prison, or other public place with detention facilities	Ss 26, 36: "pending completion of the arrangements for his deportation from Zambia at the first reasonable opportunity"; any place specially provided, a prison, or other public place with detention facilities
Zimbabwe	S 8: 14 day limit; prison, police cell or other convenient place; bond possible	S 8: "pending the completion of arrangements for the removal"; prison, police cell or other convenient place; bond possible

Table 16: Departure Regulation

SADC Country	Departure Requirements
Botswana	Production of passport and inspection by immigrtion officer (s 5)
DRC	Article 13 of Ordonnance No 87-281 du 13 Aout 1987
Lesotho	Unregulated?
Malawi	African Emigration and Immigrant Workers Act 1 of 1954
Mauritius	Production of passport to immigration officer (s 10(2) of Passport Act)
Mozambique	Passport and legal formalities (s 26)
Namibia	Departure from Namibia Regulation Amendment Act 4 of 1993 (GN 80) (GG 686 of 17 August 1993)
Seychelles	Report to Immigration officer and production of passport
South Africa	Production of passport and recorded by immigration officer (s 9(3), 9(4), 36)
Swaziland	Report of departure to immigration officer (reg 4, 5), production of passport or similar document (s 11ter of Passports Act)
Tanzania	At ports of entry and apparently reported to imagration officer (reg 20)
Zambia	Examination and production of passport (s 13)
Zimbabwe	Ports of exit, examination by immigration officer, production of valid travel document (ss 24-28)

◇ Table 17: Criminal Offences

SADC Country	Criminal Offences	Penalties and Sanctions
Botswana	Re-entry of prohibited immigrant (s 26); entrance of person endangering peace and security (s 27); aiding and abetting unlawful entry (s 28); contradictory statements (s 29); general migration offences (obstruction, forgery, false information) (s 30)	R1000 or one year or both; R4000 or 4 years or both; R1000 or one year or both; R500, one year, both; R1000 or one year.
Lesotho	Bribery (s 29); General migration offences (s 30);	R1000 or in default, five years; R1000 or in default five years;
Malawi	Re-entry of prohibited immigrant (s 35); Misuse of documents (s 36); Forgery of documents (s 37); Aiding and abetting unlawful entry (s 38); General migration offences (s 39)	Imprisonment with hard labour for three months; 250 pounds or 12 months; five years; 250 pounds or 12 months; 250 pounds or 12 months
Mauritius	Unlawful entry (s 22(a)); False answer (s 22(b)); False information (s 22I); Assisting entry or departure for money (s 22(d)); Aiding and abetting (s 22(e)); General contravention of Act (s 23)	5000 rupees or 12 months; same; same; same; 2000 rupees or 6 months
Mozambique	Clandestine migration and falsification of documents (s 41); absence of a visa or bulletin of accommodation (s 42); absence of authorization of residence (s 43); change of domicile without notification (s 44); failure to communicate the alteration of elements of identification (s 47)	Criminal Code; Daily fine of 1 m MT; Daily fine of 1 m MT; Monthly fine of 1 m MT; Daily fine of 100,00.00 MT;
Namibia	General migration offences (s 54); Aiding or abetting (s 56(a), (c)); Conveying unlawful entrants (s 56(b)); False information (s 56(d)); Falsification of	R8000 or two years or both; R20 000 or five years or both; Same; Same; Same; R8000 or two years or both

	documents (s 56(e)); Possession of official equipment, stamps (s 56(f));	
South Africa	Unlawful entry or presence (s 49(1)(a); Failure to depart (s 49(1)(b)); Assistance to enter unlawfully (s 49(2): Employment of illegal foreigner (s 49(3));	Fine or three months; Fine or nine months; Fine or one year; Fine or one year; second, two years, and third three years.
	Intentional facilitation of receipt of public services by illegal foreigner (s 49(4)); Provision of false identification by a civil servant (s 49(5); Failure to comply with civil society obligations (ss 42, 43, 44, 45, 46 read with s 49(6));	Fine; Fine and two years, if dept, ; three years Fine or 18 months; Fine or four years; Fine or one year, and
	Conspiracy to violate Act (s 49(7)); Wilfully or grossly negligent production of false certification (s 49(8); Production of purported Department document (s 49(9)); Financial offers or threats (s 49(10)); S 49(11): offence of s 37(10)?? (typographical error); Overstaying (s 50(1)) (administrative offence); Negligent incorrect certification (s 50(2))	professional suspension of two years; Fine or two years; Fine and 18 months/3 years; R3000 fine; R8000 fine.
Swaziland	False declaration or information, alteration of document, use of forged document, parting with passport, use of passport without permission (s 14(1)(a)-(f)); Refusal to leave, presence as prohibited immigrant (s 14(1)(g)-(h)); Harbouring unlawful persons (s 14(1)(i)); Corrupting an immigration officer (s 14(1)(j)); Obstruction, refusal to answer, unlawful entrance, harbouring certain persons, failure to comply with term (s 14(2)(a) -(d)); Failure to comply with	R1000 or one year; Same R500 or 6 months; Same;

	permit condition (s 14(2)(e); Unlawful employment (s 14 (2)(f)); Unlawful employment of persons (s 14(2)(g));	Same; Same
Tanzania	Failure to answer, false information, alteration of document, possession of forged document, obstruction of officer, unlawful presence, failure to leave, failure to comply with term or condition, harbouring an offender (s 31(1)); Re-entry of prohibited immigrant (s 31(3));	100 000 TS or 3 years or both; 250 000 TS or five years or both;
Zambia	Refusal to leave (s 29(1)); Unlawful entry or departure (s 29(2)); Re-entry of prohibited immigrant (s 29(3)); Refusal to obey, obstruction of officer (s 29(4), (5)); Employing a prohibited person (s 29(6)); False representations (s 29(7));	500 kwacha or 12 months or both; same; same; same; same; same;
Zimbabwe	Attempt to influence issue of a permit (s 33); Re-entry of prohibited person (s 34); Escape from lawful detention or custody (s 35); General migration offences (s 36)	1000 ZD or three years; not specified; not specified; 1000 ZD or two years or both

Table 18: Migration Source of Authority

Documents Migration 19 August 2002	Primary Source of Migration Rules	Collected Documents on Migration	Other Documents
Angola	Decree No 48/1994 of 25 November 1994 'Regulation on the Legal Regime of Foreigners' (unconfirmed)	Decree No 48/1994 of 25 November 1994 'Regulation on the Legal Regime of Foreigners' (UNHCR unofficial translation)	
Botswana	Immigration Act 19 of 1966 Last amended by Act 12 of 1991	Immigration Act 19 of 1966 as amended Immigration (Identification of Immigrants) Regulations Immigration (Visa) Regulations Immigration Regulations Immigration (Exemption) Order Immigration Points of Entry) Order Immigration (Hours of Operation) Regulations Immigration (Transfer of Minister's Powers) Regulation Employment of Non-Citizens Act 11 of 1981 as amended by Act 15 of 1981 and S.I. 59 of 1983	
Democratic Republic of Congo	Ordonnance No 87-281 du 13 Aout 1987 Portant Mesure D' Execution de l" Ordonnance-Loi No 83-033 du 12 Septembre 1983	Ordonnance No 87 -281 du 13 Aout 1987	

	relative a la Police Des Etrangers		
Lesotho	Aliens Control Act 16 of 1966 Last Amended in 1989 Passports and Travel Document Act, 1998	Aliens Control Act 16 of 1966 annotated as amended in 1989	
Malawi	Immigration Act of 1963 (Cap 15:03) Amended by Act of 1974 Immigration Amendment Act 21 of 1987	Immigration Act of 1963 as amended in 1974 Immigration Regulations Immigration Amendment Act 21 of 1987 African Emigration and Immigrant Workers Act 1 of 1954 (Cap 56:02) as last amended by GN 219 of 1964 Ministry of Home Affairs Policy Statement on Employment of Expatriates and Employment Permit Guide	
Mauritius	Immigration Act (17 May 1973) Last amended 5/83 Passport Act (14 February 1969) Deportation Act (14 December 1968) Last amended 6/83 Non-citizens (Employment Restriction) Act Government Notice 115 of 1996	Immigration Act (17 May 1973) as amended Passport Act (14 February 1969) Deportation Act (14 December 1968) as amended	
Mozambique	Law of 28 December 1993	Law of 28 December 1993 (Portuguese) Law of 28 December 1993 (unofficial English translation)	
Namibia	Immigration Control Act 7 of 1993	Immigration Control Act 7 of 1993	

		Administrator General Proclamation No. 15 of 1989	
Seychelles	Immigration Decree		
South Africa	Immigration Act 13 of 2002 (projected commencement date 1 November 2002)	Immigration Act 13 of 2002	Aliens Control Act 96 of 1991
Swaziland	Immigration Act 17 of 1982 The Passports Act 19 of 1971	Immigration Act 17 of 1982 Immigration Regulations, 1987 The Passports Act 19 of 1971	
Tanzania	Immigration Act 7 of 1995	Immigration Act 7 of 1995 Immigration Regulations, 1997 Immigration (Transitional and Savings) Order, 1997	Daily News (Tanzania), 25 May 2002
Zambia	Immigration and Deportation Act 29 of 1965 Last amended by Immigration and Deportation (Amendment) Act 31 of 1972	Immigration and Deportation Act 29 of 1965 as amended The Immigration and Deportation Regulations as amended by SI 257 of 1968 Employment Permit Requirements for Expatriate Personnel and Investors (n.d.) Guidelines on the Issuance, Extension of Permits Visa Requirements and Procedures (16 November 1998)	*Immigration and Deportation (Amendment) Act 16 of 1967 *Immigration and Deportation (Amendment) Act 31 of 1972 Immigration and Deportation (Amendment) Bill, 1997
Zimbabwe	Immigration Act 18 of 1979 Amended by S.I. 78 of 1987 Last Amended by Immigration Amendment Act 8 of 1999	Immigration Act 18 of 1979 as amended in 1987 Immigration Amendment Act 8 of 1999	Newspaper report of court order on marriage of convenience Immigration Regulations, 1998

www.ingramcontent.com/pod-product-compliance
Lightning Source LLC
Chambersburg PA
CBHW080250030426

42334CB00023BA/2766